ELEGANT
TATTING PATTERNS

Janet Carroll

DOVER PUBLICATIONS, INC.

Mineola, New York

Abbreviations

adj.	adjacent	opp	opposite
beg	beginning	OR	outer ring
bet.	between	p	picot
ch	chain	prev.	previous
cl	close	PW	press work
corr	correspond or corresponding	rep	repeat
		RW	reverse work
ctr	center	R	ring
Ctr R	center ring	RSt	roll stitch
d	double stitch or stitches	sep	separate
FW	finish work	Sh	shuttle
inc.	increase	sk	skip
IR	inner ring	smp	small picot
j	join	SR	small ring
JK	Josephine knot	sp	space
JkS	Josephine stitch	tp	tiny picot
LR	large ring	tog	together
lp	long picot		

Artwork for Figures 1–12 by Gregory Guiteras.

Published in Canada by General Publishing Company, Ltd., 30 Lesmill Road, Don Mills, Toronto, Ontario.

Published in the United Kingdom by Constable and Company, Ltd., 3 The Lanchesters, 162–164 Fulham Palace Road, London W6 9ER.

Bibliographical Note

Elegant Tatting Patterns is a new work, first published by Dover Publications, Inc., in 1996.

Library of Congress Cataloging-in-Publication Data

Carroll, Janet.
Elegant tatting patterns / Janet Carroll.
p. cm.
ISBN 0-486-29149-9 (pbk.)
1. Tatting—Patterns. I. Title.
TT840.T38C37 1996
746.43′6041—dc20
96-11632
CIP

Manufactured in the United States of America
Dover Publications, Inc., 31 East 2nd Street, Mineola, N.Y. 11501

General Instructions

Tools and Materials

There are two main types of shuttles available—one with a center shaft and one with a removable shuttle. Some shuttles have a small hook on the end for joining, but the thread can catch on the hook; a small crochet hook can be used for joining, instead. For beginners, I recommend a shuttle with a center shaft and no hook.

A smooth, tightly twisted thread is the most suitable thread for tatting. Most cotton crochet threads can be used successfully. All of the patterns in this book use DMC Cordonnet Spécial.

Winding the Shuttle

Insert the thread through the hole in the center shaft and wind the thread evenly around the shaft. Untwist the thread while winding it onto the shaft to help prevent the thread from binding while you tat. Be sure not to wind beyond the borders of the shuttle. Such overloading will damage the shuttle.

Double Stitch

The basic tatting stitch is the *double stitch*, which is worked in two parts.

Unwind the shuttle so that the thread is about 12 inches long. Hold the shuttle between the thumb and forefinger of the right hand with the thread coming from the back of the shuttle (having the thread coming from the front of the shuttle can cause knots in your work). Take the end of the thread between the thumb and forefinger of the left hand, then pass the thread around the outstretched fingers, crossing it under the thumb *(Fig. 1)*. The thread around your fingers is referred to as the *ring thread*; that coming from the shuttle is the *shuttle thread*.

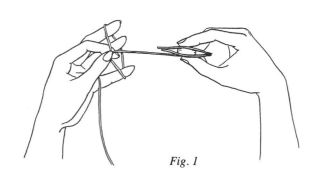

Fig. 1

With the shuttle in your right hand, pass the shuttle thread under and over this hand just behind the tips of the fingers. Pass the shuttle *under* the shuttle and ring threads between the first and second fingers of the left hand. Bring the shuttle back *over* the ring thread and under the shuttle thread *(Fig. 2)*, allowing the ring thread (the thread around the left fingers) to fall slack by bringing the four fingers of the left hand together. Pull the shuttle thread taut, causing it to form a loop around the ring thread *(Fig. 3)*. Spread the fingers of the left hand to bring the loop close to the fingers and thumb of the

left hand; pull tight. The first half of the double stitch is now complete.

The second half of the stitch is the reverse of the first. Allow the shuttle thread to fall slack, pass the shuttle *over* the ring thread, then back *under* the ring thread and *over* the shuttle thread *(Fig. 4)*. Pull the shuttle thread taut and tighten the ring thread until the second half of the stitch slips into place beside the first half. Use your right ring finger to help move the stitches into place. This completes one double stitch *(Fig. 5)*.

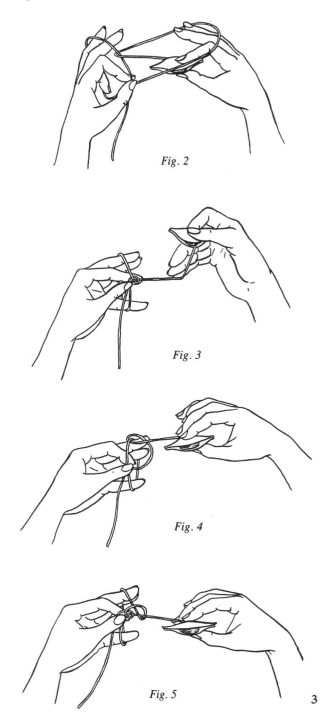

Fig. 2

Fig. 3

Fig. 4

Fig. 5

3

The double stitch should slip back and forth freely when you pull on the shuttle thread. If it does not, the stitch has been locked by a wrong motion and must be made over again (use a needle to take out the stitch). While practicing it is recommended that you take out your work occasionally; this will help you learn how the stitches are formed. Practice the doubles until you can do them without looking at the instructions. To close the ring, pull on the shuttle thread until the first and last stitches meet. Practice and have patience—your fingers are making foreign movements.

Chains are made with a shuttle and a ball thread, or with two shuttles. Tie the two threads together with a square knot, leaving 2–3-inch ends. Hold the knot in your left hand between your thumb and forefinger. Lay the ball thread over the top of your left fingers forming a half circle; then wrap it around your little finger to control the tension of the thread *(Fig. 6)*. This thread is your *chain thread* or *running line*. The double stitches are formed in the same manner as for the ring. The first double stitch should be made as close as possible to the knot.

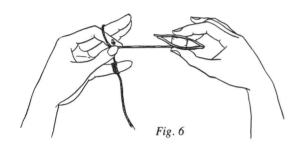

Fig. 6

Reverse Work

When working both rings and chains, you usually (although not always) reverse the work between them. Work is sometimes reversed between rings as well. To reverse the work if you have just finished a ring, turn the work over so that the bottom of the ring is at the top. Turn chains so that the stitches are upside down.

Picots

Picots are used for decoration and to join rings and chains. To form a picot, make the first half of the next double stitch; slide it on the thread, stopping about ¼ inch from the last stitch. Complete the double stitch *(Fig. 7)* and slide the entire stitch into position next to the double stitches already made. For larger picots leave a larger space between double stitches. If a picot is required at the beginning of a chain or ring, make the appropriate size picot holding it securely, then make double stitches as directed.

Fig. 7

Joining

Rings and chains are joined at picots. To join two rings, work the first ring, then work the second ring to the point it is to be joined. From the front, insert a small crochet hook (or the hook or point of the shuttle) through the last picot of the

previous ring and pull the ring thread through, making a loop large enough to insert the shuttle *(Fig. 8)*. Pass the shuttle through the loop and draw the shuttle thread tight, joining the rings. Continue making double stitches. Chains can be joined in the same way. Sometimes, it is necessary to join a chain to a

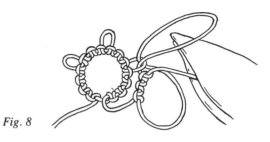

Fig. 8

ring or chain that is to the right and below the chain. In this case, insert the hook through the picot and draw up the *shuttle* thread. Pass the shuttle through the loop *(Fig. 9)*. Draw the shuttle thread tight, locking the join into position. Make sure that the stitches before the join are drawn close together, as the join will lock the stitches.

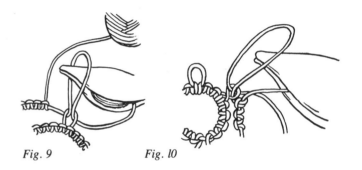

Fig. 9   Fig. l0

Joining the End to the Beginning of the Work

Work the last ring of the motif to the join; pick up the first ring, holding it so that you see the front side, fold it over to the left so that the back is now facing you. Insert the crochet hook through the picot *from the back to the front*, then twist the picot to draw the ring thread through *(Fig. 10)*. Complete the join and the ring and close the ring. When working with more than one row completed, you will find it necessary to turn the work inside out.

Joining New Thread

Always join the thread at the base of a ring or chain by making a square knot and leaving the ends until the work is finished. Do not cut the ends until later, as the strain of working may loosen the knot. Never attach a new thread in a ring, as the knots will not pass through the double stitch.

Multiple Threads

When working with two shuttles, it is important to mark the shuttles as *Sh #1* and *Sh #2*, #2 being your running line. Sh #2 will also be used to form rings on top of chains.

When working with one shuttle and a ball, the ball will always be your running line. It cannot be used to form rings.

When two colors are used in making rings, two shuttles must be used. The double stitches will be the color of the running line (the thread around your left hand). If chains appear on a two-color design, use the second shuttle as if it were a ball.

Correcting Mistakes

To correct a ring, turn the ring so the bottom of the ring is up. With the index fingers and thumbs, separate the stitches at the base of the ring. Insert a needle between the first and second halves of the last double stitch made and move the needle back and forth to loosen the stitches. Insert the needle into the second half of the last double (this is the last stitch on the ring) and pull up an excessive amount of thread. Loosen each stitch, being sure to leave a gap for each stitch. Once three or four stitches have been loosened, pull the thread from the beginning of the ring (the opposite side from where you are working). Place the ring back on your hand and continue taking off the stitches until the mistake is corrected.

Josephine Stitch and Josephine Knot

Work either the first half or the second half of the double stitch the required number of times. If worked as a ring, the resulting ring is known as a Josephine Knot.

Roll Stitch

In this stitch, the running line is wrapped around the shuttle thread, creating a smooth surface. Begin the ring and work the specified number of double stitches. Without wrapping the shuttle thread over the right hand, pass the shuttle under, then over the ring thread and away to the right *(Fig. 11)*. Keep the shuttle thread taut, causing the ring thread to wrap around the shuttle thread. Repeat the required number of times. Hold the rolled stitches securely between your thumb and forefinger and finish by working at least one double stitch. Close the ring.

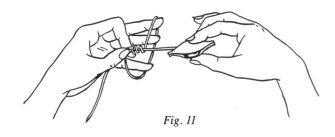

Fig. 11

Bead Work

Determine where you wish to place your beads by looking at the pattern. Before winding the shuttle, load the thread coming off of the ball with the required number of beads. Use a beading needle if the thread fits through it; if not, use no needle. Wind the shuttle, working the beads on evenly. When working chains, load the required beads onto the running line.

Working Rings: If you have three picots that require beads, push three beads up into the closed ring on your hand. *Example*—2d, p (bead), 2d, p (bead), 2d, p (bead), 2d, cl. After making 2 double stitches, pull one bead up from the ring on your hand. Make the appropriate picot, then continue making double stitches.

Working Chains: Push the required beads onto the chain thread that will be wrapped around your hand—the beads will sit on the back of your fingers. When a bead is needed, repeat as for a ring.

Weave Stitch

Load a sewing needle with approximately 12 inches of thread (the length of the thread will depend upon the size of the work). Make a slip knot in the end of the thread and insert the needle through any center picot of the work, either a ring or chain. Pass the needle through the slip knot and pull tight. Go to the opposite side of the work, insert the needle through a picot (be sure to hold your thread in the center of the work). Working back and forth, go from one picot to a picot on the opposite side. When you go through your last picot, bring the thread back to the center and wrap the thread under the center of all the threads. Weave the thread around the center numerous times, going over and under the "spokes." Insert the needle under the weaving, bring it up through the center knot and work a knot by weaving the needle through center top; cut close to work.

Finish Work

Cut the ends 3 inches long; tie them together in a square knot. Thread a needle with one end. The size of the thread will determine the size needle to use. At the base of the knot, sew the needle back through the double stitches *(Fig. 12)*. Be very careful not to pull on the double stitches, as it will stretch out your stitches. Do not run the thread through picots—the thread will show. Trim excess thread close to stitches, being careful not to cut stitches.

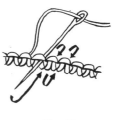

Fig. 12

Press Work

You will find it much easier if you press the work after each row after finishing the ends.

Cleaning Work

It is very important to keep your hands as clean as possible, as the thread will pick up dirt and oils from your hands.

If you are using colored thread, make sure the thread is colorfast before washing. Using a very mild, unscented liquid detergent or dish-washing soap, soak the work for several minutes. Rinse well; do not twist or wring work. Lay the work out flat on a white towel and let air dry. Sometimes pinning out the picots will help to block the work. Be sure to use rustproof straight pins. Iron your work, placing a white cotton towel between the iron and the tatted piece. Never place the iron directly on the work as this will flatten your stitches.

On hard stains, place water, detergent and piece in a clean pan. Place on stove and bring to a boil for 10 to 15 minutes, depending on the severity of the stain. Pin or lay out flat to air dry.

**CROWNING
TOUCH**

Basket of Clover

Beginner
Completed Size: 7¼″ diameter

Materials: DMC Cordonnet Spécial, size 30—1 ball each white and green 954. Two shuttles are required. Wind each shuttle with a different color. Use the white shuttle as the ring thread, the green as the chain thread.

Center Ring (white shuttle only): R 3d, smp, 6d, p, 3d, 3 p sep by 2d, 3d, p, 6d, smp, 3d, cl. *LR 3d, j to smp of last ring, 12d, 7 p sep by 2d, 12d, smp, 3d, cl. R 3d, j to smp of last ring, 6d, p, 3d, 3 p sep by 2d, 3d, p, 6d, smp, 3d, cl. Rep from * 2 times more. Rep LR once more, joining first and last smp's to first and last rings made. Cut and tie. FW.

Row 1 (white shuttle and ball): *R 4d, p, 4d, j to 4th p of LR of Ctr R, 4d, p, 4d, cl. RW. Ch 7d, p, 4d, 5 p sep by 3d, 4d, p, 7d. RW. *3-Ring Cluster*—R 8d, 3 p sep by 1d, 6d, smp, 2d, cl. R 2d, j to smp of last ring made, 8d, p, 1d, j to 3rd p of next small ring made on Ctr R, 1d, p, 8d, smp, 2d, cl. R 2d, j to smp of last ring, 6d, 3 p sep by 1d, 8d, cl. RW. Ch 7d, p, 4d, 5 p sep by 3d, 4d, p, 7d. RW. Rep from * around. J last ch to base of first ring made. Cut and tie. FW. PW.

Row 2 (2 shuttles): *R 4d, p, 4d, j to last p of ch of prev row, 2d, j to first p of next ch, 4d, p, 4d, cl. RW. Ch 8d, smp, 8d. RW. R 4d, p, 4d, j to 3rd p of same ch, 4d, p, 4d, cl. RW. Ch 8d, smp, 8d. RW. R 4d, p, 4d, j to 5th p on same ch, 4d, p, 4d, cl. RW. Ch 8d, smp, 8d. RW. Rep from * 7 times. J last ch to base of first ring. Cut and tie. FW. PW.

Row 3: *All joins will be made with the shuttle thread.* Attach white shuttle and ball thread to any p on any ch of Row 2. *Ch 8d, smp, 8d, j to free p on next ch. Rep from * around. J ch to beg. Cut and tie. FW. PW.

Row 4: Rep Row 3.

Row 5: Rep Row 3, changing smp's to p's.

Row 6 (2 shuttles): *R 2d, 3 p sep by 2d, 2d, j to p on Row 5 ch, 2d, 3 p sep by 2d, 2d, cl. RW. Ch 3d, 9 p sep by 2d, 3d. RW. Rep from * around. J last ch to base of first ring. Cut and tie. FW. PW.

Row 7 (green shuttle only): *R 1d, 11 p sep by 1d, 1d, cl. Leave ⅜″ sp, j thread to 3rd p on ch of last row, leave ⅜″ sp. R 1d, 11 p sep by 1d, 1d, cl. Leave ⅜″ sp, join to 7th p of same ch, leave ⅜″ sp. Rep from * around. J thread to base of first ring. Cut and tie. FW. PW.

Row 8 (2 shuttles): R 1d, 4 p sep by 1d, 1d, j to 5th p on ring directly above a ring of Row 6, 1d, p, 1d, j to 7th p of next ring, 1d, 4 p sep by 1d, 1d, cl. RW. *Ch 1d, 26 tp sep by 1d, 1d, twist ch 5 times. RW. R 1d, 4 p sep by 1d, 1d, j to 5th p of next ring, 1d, p, 1d, j to 7th p of next ring, 1d, 4 p sep by 1d, 1d, cl. RW. Rep from * around, omitting last ring. J last ch to first ring. Cut and tie. FW. PW.

Crowning Touch

Advanced
Completed Size: 20″ diameter

Materials: DMC Cordonnet Spécial, size 30—1 ball. Use one color only. Four shuttles are used for Rows 10 and 11. Work Rows 1 through 8 of Basket of Clover (above).

Row 9: *This row will join the remaining pairs of rings from*

Row 7. Pull a twisted ch of last row to the back of the work so that it is out of the way. *R 1d, 4 p sep by 1d, j to free 5th p of a Row 7 ring, 1d, p, 1d, j to free 7th p of next ring, 1d, 4 p sep by 1d, 1d, cl.** RW. Ch 2d, 21 p sep by 2d, 2d. RW. Pull next twisted ch to the front of the work. Rep from * to **. Pull the next twisted ch to the back of the work. Rep from * around. Cut and tie. FW. PW.

Rows 10 and 11 (4 shuttles): *Rows are worked simultaneously.* Mark shuttles in pairs (1, 1A, 2, 2A). Lay shuttle pairs out of the way when not in use. *Sh 1 and 1A: On subsequent repeats, twisted ch will lay over the top of last flat ch made.* R 1d, 4 p sep by 1d, 1d, j to 17th p on ch of last row, 1d, 4 p sep by 1d, 1d, cl. RW. Ch 1d, 19 tp sep by 1d, 1d. Twist ch 5 times. RW. *Sh 2 and 2A: Ch will lay over the top of last twisted ch made.* R 1d, 4 p sep by 1d, 1d, j to 13th p on same ch, 1d, 4 p sep by 1d, 1d, cl. RW. Ch 5d, 11 p sep by 2d, 5d. RW. *Sh 1 and 1A: Twisted ch will lay over the top of the last flat ch made.* R 1d, 4 p sep by 1d, 1d, j to 9th p on same ch, 1d, 4 p sep by 1d, 1d, cl. RW. Ch 1d, 19 tp sep by 1d, 1d. Twist ch 5 times. RW. *Sh 2 and 2A: Ch will lay over the top of last twisted ch made.* R 1d, 4 p sep by 1d, 1d, j to 5th p on same ch, 1d, 4 p sep by 1d, 1d, cl. RW. Ch 5d, 11 p sep by 2d, 5d. RW. Rep from * around, joining ch's to base of appropriate rings. Cut and tie all threads. FW. PW.

Row 12: Attach shuttle and ball thread to ctr p of any untwisted ch of last row. *Ch 10d, smp, 10d, j to ctr p of next ch. Rep from * around. Cut and tie. FW. PW.

Rows 13 and 14: Attach shuttle and ball thread to any smp of last row. *Ch 10d, smp, 10d, j to next smp. Rep from * around. Cut and tie. FW. PW.

Row 15: Attach shuttle and ball thread to any p of last row. *Ch 6d, 5 p sep by 3d, 6d, j to next p. Rep from * around. Cut and tie. FW. PW.

Row 16: *5 Ring Cluster*—R 14d, 7 p sep by 1d, 8d, smp, 6d, cl. R 6d, j to smp of last ring, 4d, 5 p sep by 1d, 4d, smp, 6d, cl. R 6d, j to smp, 8d, 7 p sep by 1d, 8d, smp, 6d, cl. R 6d, j to smp, 4d, 5 p sep by 1d, 4d, smp, 6d, cl. R 6d, j to smp, 8d, 7 p sep by 1d, 14d, cl.* RW. Ch 40d, smp, 10d. RW. Rep from * to * once. RW. Ch 10, j to smp of last ch, 40d. RW. Rep from * to * once. **Ch 20d. RW. JK 6, j to 3rd p of adj ring of last cluster, JK6, cl. RW. Ch 5d, j to first p of ch on Row 15, 2d, 3 p sep by 2d, 2d, j to 5th p of next ch, 5d. RW. JK 6, j to 5th p of same ring as last JK, JK6, cl. RW. (Ch 5d, 5 p sep by 2d, 5d. RW. JK 6, j to 2nd p of next ring, JK6, cl. RW. Ch 5d, 5 p sep by 2d, 5d. RW. JK 6, j to 3d p of same ring as last JK, JK6, cl. RW. Ch 5d, 5 p sep by 2d, 5d. RW. JK 6, j to 4th p of next ring, JK6, cl. RW. Ch 5d, 5 p sep by 2d, 5d. RW. JK 6, j to 5th p of same ring, JK6, cl. RW) twice, joining first p of last ch to 4th p of adj ring of next 5-Ring Cluster. Ch 20d, j in base of first cluster. Cut and tie. Attach thread to base of first 5-Ring Cluster and rep from **, skipping one joining on Row 15 and joining to next 2 chs and joining 5th p of last ch to 4th p of adj ring of next cluster. FW. PW. Make 7 more points, following picture for spacing. There will be 2 free chs bet points.

Row 17: *R 1d, 3 p sep by 1d, 1d, j to 4th p on first free ch to right of point, 1d, 3 p sep by 1d, 1d, cl. RW. Ch 1d, 19 smp sep by 1d, 1d, twist ch 9 times. RW. Rep ring and ch, joining to 4th p of next ch of Row 15. Sk first free ch of point. Rep ring and ch, joining rings to the 4th p of each of the next 5 ch's.

(Continued on page 9)

Carousel

Over/Under

Crisscross

Chicken Eggs
Advanced

Materials: DMC Cordonnet Spécial, size 30—one ball will make several eggs; large chicken eggs; nail or large needle; jewelry finding—one small "cap" with ring; epoxy glue; clear spray varnish; toothpick; nylon scrubbing pad; cord for hanging.

Prepare Egg: Gently scrub exterior of egg with nylon scrubbing pad. With nail or needle, make a tiny hole in wide end of egg. In opposite end of egg, make a hole at least ⅛″ in diameter (be careful not to make the hole larger than the "cap" you are using). Insert sharp object into the egg to break up the yolk. Blow through the small hole to empty the egg. Wash out the egg thoroughly with hot soapy water; allow it to "drip dry." Varnish the egg following the instructions on the can. Glue the cap over the hole. Varnish the egg and allow to dry. Attach the hanging cord.

Carousel

Row 1 (one shuttle): SR 1d, 4 p sep by 1d, 1d, cl. RW. ¼″ sp. R 4d, p, 4d, smp, 4d, p, 4d, cl. RW. ¼″ sp. *SR 1d, j to corr p of last SR, 1d, 3 p sep by 1d, 1d, cl. RW. ¼″ sp. R 4d, j to corr p, 4d, p, 4d, p, 4d, cl. RW. Rep from * 12 times, joining last 2 rings to corr p's on first 2 rings. ¼″ sp. J to base of first SR. Cut and tie. FW.

Row 2 (2 shuttles): J thread to joining bet any 2 large rings. *Sh 1:* *Ch 3d, p, 1d, p, 1d. *Sh 2:* JK 10. *Sh 1:* Ch 1d, p, 1d, p, 3d. J to next joining on Row 1. Rep from * around. Cut and tie. FW.

Row 3 (2 shuttles): J thread to any two adj chs of last row, joining in last p of one ch and first p of next. *Sh 1:* *Ch 6d, p (you may need lp for fatter eggs), 1d, 2 p sep by 1d, 1d. *Sh 2:* JK 10. Sh 1: Ch 1d, 3 p sep by 1d, 6d. J to next pair of adj ch's as before. Rep from * around. Cut and tie. FW.

Row 4 (2 shuttles): J thread to two adj chs of Row 3 as before. *Sh 1:* *Ch 6d, p, 1d, p, 1d. *Sh 2:* JK 10. *Sh 1:* Ch 1d, p, 1d, p, 6d. J to next pair of adj chs as before. Rep from * around. Cut and tie. FW.

Row 5 (one shuttle): R 4d, j to first p on first ch made on last row, 3d, smp, 3d, j to last p on next ch, 4d, cl. RW. ¼″ sp. R 4d, lp, 3d, smp, 3d, lp, 4d, cl. RW. ¼″sp. *R 4d, j to first p on same ch as last joining (after JK), 3d, smp, 3d, j to 4th p on next ch, 4d. RW. ¼″ sp. R 4d, lp, 3d, smp, 3d, lp, 4d, cl. RW. ¼″ sp. Rep from * around. J to base of first ring. Cut and tie. FW.

Row 6 (2 shuttles): J thread to any two adj rings of last row, joining to last lp of one and first lp of next. *Sh 1:* *Ch 4d, p, 1d, p, 1d. *Sh 2:* JK3, smp, JK3, cl. *Sh 1:* Ch 1d, p, 1d, p, 4d. J to next lp of same ring and lp of next ring as before. Rep from * around, join last ch in first join. Cut and tie. FW. If necessary, rep Row 6 for larger eggs.

Row 7: R 3d, j to corr p of any JK on last row, 3d, cl. RW. *Ch 1d, 11 p sep by 1d, 1d. RW. Twist ch 5 times. R 3d, j to corr p of next ring, 3d, cl. RW. Rep from * around, joining last ch in base of first ring. Cut and tie. FW.

Base—Row 8 (2 shuttles): *Base is made separately and joined on next row. Sh 1:* LR 4d, p, 3d, smp, 3d, p, 4d, cl. RW. *Sh 2:* JK10. RW. *Sh 1:* R 4d, j to 3rd p on LR, 3d, smp, 3d, p, 4d, cl. RW. *Sh 2:* JK 10. RW. Rep from * 5 times, joining 3rd p on 5th ring to first p on first ring made. Cut and tie. FW.

Row 9 (2 shuttles): J thread to ctr p on any ch of Row 7. *Sh 1:* *Ch 1d, 10 p sep by 1d, 1d, twist ch 5 times. *Sh 2:* JK 10. *Sh 1:* Ch 1d, 10 p sep by 1d, 1d, twist ch 5 times. J to ctr p on next ch of Row 7. Ch 1d, 5 p sep by 1d, 1d, twist ch 3 times. *Sh 2:* R 3d, j to corr smp on Row 8, 3d, cl. *Sh 1:* Ch 1d, 5 p sep by 1d, 1d, twist ch 3 times. J in ctr p on next ch of Row 7. Rep from * around. After joining 3rd rings together, slip piece over egg; continue working pattern on egg. Cut and tie. FW.

Over/Under

Row 1: *3-Ring Cluster*—R 1d, 3 p sep by 1d, 1d, smp, 1d, cl. R 1d, j to smp, 1d, 3 p sep by 1d, 1d, smp, 1d, cl. R 1d, j to smp, 1d, 3 p sep by 1d, 1d, cl. RW. Ch 2d, smp, 1d, 3 p sep by 1d, 1d, smp, 2d. RW. *3-Ring Cluster*—R 1d, p, 1d, j to corr p of last ring, 1d, p, 1d, smp, 1d, cl. R 1d, j to smp, 1d, 3 p sep by 1d, 1d, smp, 1d, cl. R 1d, j to smp, 1d, 3 p sep by 1d, 1d, cl. RW. Ch 2d, j to corr smp of last ch, 1d, 3 p sep by 1d, 1d, smp, 2d. RW. Rep from * 5 or 6 times depending on size of egg, joining last ring and ch to first ring and ch. J last ch to base of first cluster. Cut and tie. FW.

Row 2: *Note—You will work around piece 3 times.* J thread to first free p of 2nd ring of any cluster. *Ch 4d, 3 p sep by 2d, 4d, j to first free p on 2nd ring of next cluster. Rep from * around. J last ch to *2nd p* of first cluster. Folding prev chs out of the way, **ch 6d, 3 p sep by 2d, 6d, j to 2nd p on 2nd ring of next cluster. Rep from ** around. J last ch to *3rd p* of first cluster joined. ***Ch 5d, 3 p sep by 2d, 5d, j to 3rd p on 2nd ring of next cluster. Rep from *** around. J last ch to base of first ch. Cut and tie. FW.

Row 3: R 1d, 3 p sep by 1d, 1d, j to adj p's of 3rd and first rings of any two adj clusters of Row 1, 1d, 3 p sep by 1d, 1d, cl. RW. *Ch 12d, 3 p sep by 2d, 12d. RW. Skip one set of adj p's. R 1d, 3 p sep by 1d, j to next adj p's, 1d, 3 p sep by 1d, 1d, cl. RW.* Rep from * to * twice—3 ch's with 3 p's. **Ch 14d, p, 14d. RW. R 1d, 3 p sep by 1d, 1d, j to next free adj rings, 1d, 4 p sep by 1d, 1d, cl. Rep from ** around. J last ch to base of first ring made. Cut and tie. FW.

Row 4: *Note: You will probably have 2 identical ch's next to one another at some point on the piece.* R 1d, 4 p sep by 1d, 1d, j to ctr p of any 3-p ch, 1d, 3 p sep by 1d, 1d, cl. RW. *Ch 8d, p, 4d, p, 8d. RW. R 1d, 3 p sep by 1d, 1d, j to single p on next ch, 1d, 3 p sep by 1d, 1d. RW. Ch 8d, p, 4d, p, 8d. RW. R 1d, 3 p sep by 1d, 1d, j to ctr p of next 3-p ch. RW. Rep from * around. J last ch to base of first ring. Cut and tie. FW.

Row 5: R 1d, 3 p sep by 1d, 1d, j to 2nd p on first ch made on last row, 1d, 3 p sep by 1d, 1d, cl. RW. *Ch 3d, p, 3d. RW. R 1d, p, 1d, j to corr p of last ring, 1d, p, 1d, j to first p on same ch, 1d, 3 p sep by 1d, 1d, cl. RW. Ch 8d. RW. *3-Ring Cluster*—R 1d, p, 1d, j to corr p on last ring, 1d, p, 1d, smp, 1d, cl. R 1d, j to smp, 1d, 3 p sep by 1d, 1d, smp, 1d, cl. R 1d, j to smp, 1d, 3 p sep by 1d, 1d, cl. Ch 8d.† RW. R 1d, p, 1d, j to corr p, 1d, p, 1d, j to 2nd p on next ch, 1d, 3 p sep by 1d, 1d, cl. RW. Rep from * around, ending last rep at † and joining last ring to first ring. J last ch to base of first ring. Cut and tie. FW.

Row 6: R 1d, 7 p sep by 1d, 1d, cl. RW. Ch 12d, j to first ch made on last row, 12d. RW. *R 1d, 7 p sep by 1d, 1d, cl. RW. Ch 12d, skip 2 ch's, j to next picot ch, 12d. Rep from * around. J last ch to base of first ring. Cut and tie. FW.

Row 7: Rep Row 1.

Row 8: Rep Row 2.

Row 9: Slip piece over egg and work as follows: R 1d, 3 p sep by 1d, 1d, j to adj p's bet 3rd and first rings on joined clusters, 1d, 3 p sep by 1d, 1d, cl. RW. *Ch 14d, j to 4th p on corr ring of Row 6 (skip every other ring), 14d. RW. R 1d, 3 p sep by 1d, 1d, (skip one set of clusters), j bet next set of clusters, 1d, 3 p sep by 1d, 1d, cl. Rep from * 2 times. **Ch 10d, p, 2d, j to 4th p on corr free alternating ring, 2d, p, 10d. RW. R 1d, 3 p sep by 1d, 1d, j bet next free set of alternating clusters, 1d, 3 p sep

by 1d, 1d, cl. RW. Rep from ** until all clusters and rings are joined, omitting last ring and joining last ch to base of first ring made. Cut and tie. FW.

Crisscross

Top Half—Row 1: R 6d, 3 smp sep by 6d, 6d, cl. RW. *Ch 2d. RW. R 20d, cl. RW. Ch 2d. RW. R 6d, j to 3rd smp on next to last ring, 6d, 2 smp sep by 6d, 6d, cl. Rep from * 7 times, joining last ring to first ring—9 joined rings and 9 free rings. Cut and tie. FW.

Row 2: R 12d, p, 12d. RW. Ch 6d, j to any free p on last row, 6d. RW. *R 12d, p, 12d, cl. RW. Ch 6d, j to next free p on last row, 6d. Rep from * around. Join last ch to base of first ring made. Cut and tie. FW.

Row 3: J thread to any free p on last row. Ch 2, smp, 3d, 7 p sep by 2d, 3d, smp, 2d. *J to next corr p of last row. Ch 2d, j to corr smp of last ch, 2d, 7 p sep by 2d, 3d, smp, 2d. Rep from * around. J last ch to first ch. J to base of first ch. Cut and tie. FW.

Lower Half: Rep Rows 1–3 of Top Half.

Center Fill-in: Place Top and Lower Halves over egg, aligning rings and ch's. Thread a needle with a long length of thread. Join thread to 2nd free p of any ch at top; begin weaving down to 6th free p of opposite ch, up to next 2nd p and down to 6th; continue on around. Once around, leave plenty of thread to work with, then turn egg over and rep the process.

Crowning Touch

(Continued from page 7)

Skip to 2nd 5-Ring Cluster made. Rep ring and ch, j next ring to 2nd p of first free ring. Skip to the next ring, j to 2nd p and 6th p (2 rings). Join next ring to the 4th p of next ring. Work down opp side of point; j all rings to 2nd p's to corr with first side. Next ring will attach to 4th p of next free ch of Row 15. Rep ch. Rep from * around. Cut and tie. FW. PW.

Row 18: Starting on the same ch as on Row 17, *R 1d, 3 p sep by 1d, j to 2nd p of ch, 1d, p, 1d, j to 2nd p of adj ring of last row, 1d, p, 1d, cl. RW. Ch 6d, 9 p sep by 2d, 6d, RW. *Lift twisted ch up out of the way.* R 1d, 3 p sep by 1d, 1d, j to 2nd p of next ch, 1d, p, 1d, j to 2nd p of adj ring, 1d, p, 1d, cl. RW. Ch 6d, 9 p sep by 2d, 6d. RW. *Pull twisted ch down out of the way.* Skip first ch on point. **R 1d, 3 p sep by 1d, 1d, j to 2nd p on next ch, 1d, 3 p sep by 1d, 1d, cl. RW. Ch 6d, 9 p sep by 2d, 6d. RW. *Lift twisted ch up out of way.* Alternately lowering and lifting twisted chs on remainder of row, rep from ** 4 times. R 1d, 3 p sep by 1d, 1d, j to 3rd p of next ch, 1d, 3 p sep by 1d, 1d, cl. Rep ch. Skip to 2nd 5-Ring Cluster made. R 1d, p, 1d, j to 6th p on adj ring of Row 17, 1d, p, 1d, j to 4th p on 5-Cluster Ring, 1d, 3p sep by 1d, 1d, cl. Ch 6d, 9 p sep by 2d, 6d. RW. R 1d, p, 1d, j to 2nd p on adj ring, 1d, p, 1d, j to 4th p on corr ring of cluster, 1d, p, 1d, j to corr p of adj ring, 1d, p, 1d, cl. RW. Ch 6d, 9 p sep by 2d, 6d. RW. R 1d, 3 p sep by 1d, 1d, j to 2nd p on next ring, 1d, 3 p sep by 1d, 1d, cl. RW. Ch 6d, 9 p sep by 2d, 6d. RW. Work down opp side of point to corr with first side. Remember to lift and lower twisted ch's so that flat ch's will go over and under. Rep from * around. Cut and tie. FW. PW.

RISING STAR

POINT OF LIGHT
INSTRUCTIONS ON PAGE 12.

Rising Star

Intermediate
Completed size: 16″ diameter

Materials: DMC Cordonnet Spécial, size 30—one ball.

Row 1: (R 5d, 3 p sep by 2d, 5d, smp, 8d, cl. RW.) 2 times. Ch 1d, 9 smp sep by 1d, 1d, twist ch 4 times. RW. *R 8d, j to smp of corr ring, 5d, 3 p sep by 2d, 5d, cl. RW. R 5d, 3 p sep by 2d, 5d, smp, 8d, cl. RW. Ch 1d, 9 smp sep by 1d, 1d, twist ch 4 times. Rep from * 15 times, joining corr p of last ring to first ring. J ch to beg. Cut and tie. FW. PW.

Row 2: *All joins are made with the shuttle thread.* Join thread bet any set of joined rings on outside of work. *Ch 9d, p, 7d, j to 2nd p on ring, 7d, j to ctr p on twisted ch, 7d, j to 2nd p of next ring, 7d, p, 9d, j bet next 2 rings. Rep from * around. J last ch to beg. Cut and tie. FW. PW.

Row 3: *5-Ring Cluster*—R 16d, smp, 2d, cl. SR 2d, j to smp, 4d, smp, 2d, cl. LR 2d, j to smp, 10d, j to same joining as last row's ch to twisted ch, 10d, smp, 2d, cl. SR 2d, j to smp, 4d, smp, 2d, cl. R 2d, j to smp, 16d, cl. RW. Ch 8d, p, 8d, smp, 2d. RW. *3-Ring Cluster*—R 10d, j to p on next ch of last row, 8d, smp, 2d, cl. R 2d, j to smp, 6d, p, 6d, smp, 2d, cl. R 2d, j to smp, 8d, p, 10d, cl. RW. Ch 2d, j to corr smp of last ch made, 18d, smp, 2d. RW. *3-Ring Cluster*—R 10d, j to corr p of last ring made, 8d, smp, 2d, cl. R 2d, j to smp, 6d, p, 6d, smp, 2d, cl. R 2d, j to smp, 8d, p, 10d, cl. RW. Ch 2d, j to smp of last ch, 18d, smp, 2d. RW. *3-Ring Cluster*—R 10d, j to corr p, 8d, smp, 2d, cl. R 2d, j to smp, 6d, p, 6d, smp, 2d, cl. R 2d, j to smp, 18d, cl. RW. Ch 2d, j to smp, 13d, smp, 13d, smp, 2d. RW. *3-Ring Cluster*—R 12d, smp, 2d, cl. LR 2d, j to smp, 10d, j to free p of last 3-Ring Cluster, 10d, smp, 2d, cl. R 2d, j to smp, 12d, cl. RW. Ch 2d, j to smp, 13d, smp, 13d, smp, 2d. RW. *3-Ring Cluster*—R 18d, smp, 2d, cl. R 2d, j to smp, 6d, j in corr p (this makes 3 3-Ring Clusters joined tog), 6d, smp, 2d, cl. R 2d, j to smp, 8d, p, 10d, cl. RW. Ch 2d, j to smp, 18d, smp, 2d. RW. *3-Ring Cluster*—R 10d, j to corr p, 8d, smp, 2d, cl. R 2d, j to smp, 6d, j to corr p on cluster opposite, 6d, smp, 2d, cl. R 2d, j to smp, 8d, p, 10d, cl. RW. Ch 2d, j to smp, 18d, smp, 2d. RW. *3-Ring Cluster*—R 10d, j to corr p, 8d, smp, 2d, cl. R 2d, j to smp, 6d, j to corr p on cluster opposite, 6d, smp, 2d, cl. R 2d, j to corr p on next ch of last row, 10d, cl. RW. Ch 2d, j to smp of last ch, 8d, p, 8d. RW. Rep from * 7 times. J last ch to base of first cluster. Cut and tie. FW. PW.

Row 4: *All joins are made with the shuttle thread.* Join thread to first p made on ch above 5-Ring Cluster. *Ch 2d, p, 2d, j to next p on opp side of 5-Ring Cluster. Ch 20d, skip first 3-Ring Cluster and j over the p joining of ch on last row. Ch 20, j in next p joining. Ch 15, j in smp, 15d, j in p joining, 15d, j in smp, 15d, j in p joining, 20d, j in next p joining, 20d, skip one 3-Ring Cluster, j in next p over 5-Ring Cluster. Rep from * 7 times. Cut and tie. FW. PW.

Row 5: *Join all ch's in corr joinings as on last row.* Join thread to smp of any small ch over 5-Ring Cluster. *Ch 8d, p, 12d, j, 20d, j, (17d, j) 4 times, 20d, j, 12d, p, 8d, j in p on next small ch. Rep from * around. Cut and tie. FW. PW.

Row 6: *5-Ring Cluster*—*R 23d, smp, 2d, cl. SR 2d, j to smp, 8d, smp, 2d, cl. LR 2d, j to smp, 11d, j to first free p on last row, 8d, j to free p on next ch, 11d, smp, 2d, cl. SR 2d, j to smp, 8d, smp, 2d, cl. R 2d, j to smp, 23d, cl. RW. Ch 12d, p, 10d, j bet ch-20 and ch-17 of last row, (17d, j in corr joining of last row) 4 times, 10d, p, 12d. RW. Rep from * 7 times. J last ch to base of first cluster. Cut and tie. FW. PW.

Row 7: *3-Ring Cluster*—LR 14d, j to free p on ch before 5-Ring Cluster, 12d, smp, 2d, cl. R 2d, j to smp, 7d, p, 7d, smp, 2d, cl. LR 2d, j to smp, 12d, p, 14d, cl. RW. Ch 2d, smp, 22d, smp, 2d. RW. ***3-Ring Cluster*—LR 14d, j to corr p of last LR made, 12d, smp, 2d, cl. R 2d, j to smp, 7d, p, 7d, smp, 2d, cl. LR 2d, j to smp, 12d, p, 14d, cl. RW. Ch 2, j to corr smp of last ch made, 22d, smp, 2d. RW.** Rep from ** to ** twice. *3-Ring Cluster*— LR 14d, j to corr p of last LR, 12d, smp, 2d, cl. R 2d, j to smp, 7d, p, 7d, smp, 2d, cl. LR 2d, j to smp, 26d, cl. RW. Ch 2d, j to corr p of last ch made, 18d, smp, 18d, smp, 2d. RW. *3-Ring Cluster*—SR 12d, smp, 2d, cl. LR 2d, j to smp, 12d, j to corr p of last cluster made, 12d, smp, 2d, cl. SR 2d, j to smp, 12d, cl. RW. Ch 2d, j to smp, 18d, smp, 18d, smp, 2d. RW. *3-Ring Cluster*—LR 26d, smp, 2d, cl. R 2d, j to smp, 7d, j in corr p across (as joining of last group of rings), 7d, smp, 2d, cl. LR 2d, j to smp, 12d, p, 14d, cl. RW. Ch 2d, j to corr smp, 22d, smp, 2d. RW. Rep ** to ** 2 times, joining corr p's to clusters on opp side. Rep once more, omitting last ch and joining last p of last ring to p of next ch on last row. RW. Ch 2d, j to corr smp of last ch, 16d, smp, 2d, j bet the first and 2nd ch-17 of last row. Ch 2d, j to smp of last ch made, 16d, smp, 16d, smp, 8d, smp, 4d. RW. *5-Ring Cluster*—R 22d, smp, 2d, cl. SR 2d, j to smp, 8d, smp, 2d, cl. LR 2d, j to smp, 14d, j bet next set of ch-17's of last row, 14d, smp, 2d, cl. SR 2d, j to smp, 8d, smp, 2d, cl. R 2d, j to smp, 22d, cl. RW. Ch 4d, j to corr smp of last ch made, 8d, smp, 16d, smp, 16d, smp, 2d, j bet last group of ch-17's of last row. Ch 2d, j to smp of last ch made, 16d, smp, 2d. Rep from * around, joining last ch to first ch and to base of first cluster. Cut and tie. FW. PW.

Row 8: Join shuttle and ball threads to p joining above first 3-Ring Cluster made on last row. *(Ch 23d, j over joining p on corr ch's) 3 times, 20d, j in corr smp, 20d, j in next p joining, 20d, j in next smp, 20d, j in next p joining, (23d, j as before) 3 times. Ch 28d, j in first smp on ch over 5-Ring Cluster, 12d, smp, 8d, j in next smp, 11d, smp, 11d, j in next smp, 8d, smp, 12d, j in next smp, 28d, j over next 3-Ring Cluster. Rep from * around. Cut and tie. FW. PW.

Row 9: J thread on left side of a Row 7 "spoke" bet ch's over 3rd set of 3-Ring Clusters. *Ch 25d, j bet next ch's. Ch 22d, j as before, rep last ch 3 times, ch 25d, j, 15d, smp, 15d, j in next free smp, 20d, j in next free p, 20d, j in free p, 15d, smp, 15d. Rep from * around. *Do not cut thread.*

Row 10: Starting directly over and in the same manner as beginning of prev row, *ch 25d, j bet next ch's. Rep from * 5 times. Ch 15d, j in smp, 15d, j bet next corr ch's, 24d, j as before, 24d, j as before, 15d, j in smp, 15d, j as before. Rep from * around. Cut and tie. FW. PW.

Point of Light

Intermediate
(Shown on page 10)
Completed size: 25" diameter

Materials: DMC Cordonnet Spécial—one ball white and one ball blue. Use white shuttle and ball unless otherwise directed.

Center Ring (white shuttle only): R 2d, 12p sep by 3d, 1d, cl. Cut and tie. FW.

Row 1 (blue shuttle and white ball): *R 3d, lp, 3d, cl. RW. Ch 3d, j to p on Ctr R, 3d. RW. Rep from * around, joining ch's to corr p's, and last ch to base of first ring made. Cut and tie. FW.

Row 2 (blue shuttle and white ball): *R 3d, j to any lp, 3d, cl. RW. Ch 3d, 4 p sep by 2d, 3d. RW. Rep from * around, joining rings to corr p's and last ch to base of first ring made. Cut and tie. FW. PW.

Row 3: *All joins are made with the shuttle thread.* J thread to first p made on any ch. *Ch 4d, j to 4th p on next ch, 7d, smp, 5d, j in next free p, 5d, j to corr smp on last ch, 3d, smp, 3d, smp, 5d, j in next free p, 5d, j to corr smp on last ch, 7d, j in next free p. Rep from * around. Join last ch to first ch made. Cut and tie. FW. PW.

Row 4 (2 shuttles, Sh 1 is blue, Sh 2 is white): *Sh 1:* R 7d, j to first free p on Row 3, 7d, cl. RW. *Ch 10d. Sh 2:* JK 12. *Sh 1:* Ch 3d, p, 3d. *Sh 2:* JK 12. *Sh 1:* Ch 10d. RW. R 7d, j to next free p on Row 3, 7d. RW. Rep from * around, omitting last ring. J last ch to base of first ring. Cut and tie. FW. PW.

Row 5 (2 shuttles): *Use Sh 2 for all JK's on row unless otherwise indicated.* *R 9d, j to free p bet 2 JK's, 9d, cl. RW. Ch 10d. (JK 10. Ch 3d.) twice. JK 10. Ch 4d, smp, 2d. RW. JK 10 with Sh 1. RW. Ch 2d, j to smp of last ch, 4d. (JK 10. Ch 3d.) twice. JK 10. Ch 10d. Rep from * around. Join ch to beg. Cut and tie. FW. PW.

Row 6: J thread in joining over Sh-1 JK on last row. *Ch 6d, 7 smp sep by 6d, 6d, j in smp joining over next Sh-1 JK on last row, 6d, j in next free smp. Rep from * around. J last ch to base of first ch. Cut and tie. FW. PW.

Row 7: J thread to last smp of last row. *Ch 6d, j to first smp of next ch, **4d, smp, 4d, j to next free smp, rep from ** 5 times. Rep from * around. J last ch to base of first ch. Cut and tie. FW. PW.

Row 8: J thread to last smp on last row. *Ch 2d, p, 2d, j to first free p on next set of chains, **4d, smp, 4d, j to next free p. Rep from ** 4 times. Rep from * around. J last ch to base of first ch. Cut and tie. FW. PW.

Row 9: J thread to last smp on last row. *Ch 3d, smp, 3d, j to first smp of next ch set, **5d, smp, 5d, j to next smp. Rep from ** 3 times. Rep from * around. J last ch to base of first ch. Cut and tie. FW. PW.

Row 10 (blue shuttle and white ball): *JK 6, j to first smp made on last row, JK 6, cl. RW. Ch 4d, smp, 2d, j to next free smp, **5d, smp, 5d, j to next free smp, rep from ** 2 times. Ch 2d, smp, 4d. Rep from * around. J last ch to base of first ring made. Cut and tie. FW. PW.

Row 11: J thread to last smp made. *Ch 5d, smp, 5d, j to next smp. Rep from * around. J last ch to base of first ch. Cut and tie. FW. PW.

Row 12: J thread to first smp made on last row. *Ch 6d, smp, 6d, j to next smp. Rep from * around. J last ch to base of first ch. Cut and tie. FW. PW.

Rows 13–18: Repeat Row 12.

Row 19 (blue shuttle and white ball): R 12d, j to first smp made on last row, 12d, cl. RW. *Ch 5d, 4 smp sep by 2d, 5d. RW. R 12d, j to next smp on last row, 12d, cl. Rep from * around, omitting last ring. J last ch to base of first ring made. Cut and tie. FW. PW.

Row 20: J thread to first smp made on last row. *Ch 7d, smp, 5d, j to next smp of last row, 5d, j to last smp made, 6d, smp, 5d, j to next smp on last row, 5d, j to last smp made, 7d, j to next smp on last row, 3d, lp, 3d, j to next free smp on last row. Rep from * around. J last ch to base of first ch. Cut and tie. FW. PW.

Row 21: J thread to first lp made on last row. Ch 3d, smp, *10d, 4 smp sep by 2d, 10d†, smp, 3d, j to next lp, 3d, j to last smp made. Rep from * around, ending last rep at †. Join last smp to beg smp, ch 3. Join to beg of row. Cut and tie. FW. PW.

Row 22: J thread to first smp on ch of last row. *Ch 7d, smp, 5d, j to next free smp on last row, 5d, j to last smp made, 6d, smp, 5d, j to next free smp on last row, 5d, j to last smp made, 6d, j to next free smp on last row, 5d, lp, 5d, j to first smp of next set. Rep from * around. J last ch to base of first ch. Cut and tie.

Row 23: J thread to first lp made on last row. Ch 3d, smp, *7d, 3 smp sep by 5d, 7d, smp, 3d, j to next lp,† 3d, join to last smp made. Rep from * around, ending last rep at † and joining last smp to beg smp. Cut and tie. FW. PW.

Row 24: J thread to first free smp made on last row. *Ch 7d, smp, 5d, j to next smp on last row, 5d, smp, 7d, j to next smp on last row, 4d, j to first smp of next set. Rep from * around. J last ch to base of first ch. Cut and tie. FW. PW.

Row 25: J thread to first smp made on last row. *Ch 7d, smp, 7d, j to next free smp on last row. Rep from * around. J last ch to beg. Cut and tie. FW. PW.

Rows 26–33: Rep Row 25 (omit every 10th p on Row 33).

Row 34—First Point: J thread to first smp made on last row. (Ch 8d, smp, 8d, j to next free smp) 7 times. Ch 16d, j to next free smp. RW. Ch 20d, smp, 10d, j to next free corr smp, (10d, smp, 10d, j to next smp) 5 times. Ch 20d, j to last free corr smp. RW. Ch 24d, smp, 12d, j to corr smp, (12d, smp, 12d, j to next smp) 4 times. Ch 24d, j to last corr p. RW. Ch 28d, smp, 14d, j to corr smp, (14d, smp, 14d, j) 3 times, 28d, j to corr smp. RW. Ch 32d, smp, 16d, j to corr smp, (16d, smp, 16d, j) twice, ch 32d, j to corr smp. RW. Ch 36d, smp, 18d, j to corr smp, 18d, smp, 18d, j to corr smp, 36d, j to corr smp. RW. Ch 40d, smp, 20d, j to corr smp, 40d, j to corr smp. RW. Ch 70d, j to corr smp. Cut and tie. Skip one ch on Row 33. Attach thread and rep Row 34. Rep until 12 points have been made.

Emily

Intermediate
Completed size: 7½″ diameter

Materials: DMC Cordonnet Spécial, size 30—one ball.
Use shuttle and ball unless otherwise directed.

Center Ring (one shuttle): R 2d, 12 p sep by 3d, 1d, cl. Cut and tie. FW. PW.

Row 1: R 4d, lp (leave ½" sp for p), 4d, cl. RW. Ch 4d, j to any p on Ctr R, 4d. RW. *R 4d, lp, 4d, cl. Ch 4d, j to next free p on Ctr R, 4d. RW. Rep from * 10 times, j last ch to base of first ring made. Cut and tie. FW. PW.

Row 2: R 4d, j to any lp of last row, 4d, cl. RW. Ch 4d, 4 smp sep by 2d, 4d. RW. *R 4d, j to next lp, 4d, cl. Ch 4d, 4 smp sep by 2d, 4d. RW. Rep from * 10 times. J last ch to base of first ring made. Cut and tie. FW. PW.

Row 3: Join ball and shuttle threads to first p made on last row. *Ch 12d, j in 2nd smp of same ch, 7d, smp, 7d, j in 3rd smp, 12d, j in 4th smp, 6d, j in first p of next ch. Rep from * around. J to first p. Cut and tie. FW. PW.

Row 4 (2 Shuttles): *Sh 1: 3-Ring Cluster—R 12d, smp, 2d, cl. R 2d, j to smp, 9d, j to free smp on ch of last row, 9d, smp, 2d, cl. R 2d, j to smp, 12d, cl. RW. Ch 10d. Sh 2: JK 12. Sh 1: Ch 6d, smp, 6d. Sh 2: JK 12. Sh 1: Ch 10d. RW. Rep from * around. J last ch to base of first 3-Ring Cluster made. Cut and tie. FW. PW.

Row 5 (2 Shuttles): *Sh 1: 3-Ring Cluster—R 12d, smp, 2d, cl. R 2d, j to smp, 9d, j to p bet JK rings of Row 4, 9d, smp, 2d, cl. R 2d, j to smp, 12d, cl. RW. Ch 8d. (Sh 2: JK 12. Sh 1: Ch 4d.) twice. Sh 2: JK 12. Sh 1: Ch 6d, smp, 2d. RW. R 10d, cl. RW. Ch 2d, j to corr p of prev ch, 6d. (Sh 2: JK 12. Sh 1: Ch 4d.) twice. Sh 2: JK 12. Sh 1: Ch 8d. RW. Rep from * around. J to base of first 3-Ring Cluster made. Cut and tie. FW. PW.

Row 6: J thread in base of any 3-Ring Cluster. *Ch 6d, smp (j to last smp of prev ch on following repeats), 5d, 5 smp sep by 5d, 6d, j in p joining above 10d ring, 6d, j in corr smp on ch just made, 5d, 5 smp sep by 5d, 6d, j in base of 3-Ring Cluster. Rep from * around, joining last ch to first smp made; join to base of first 3-Ring Cluster. Cut and tie. FW. PW.

Row 7: J thread to first free smp made on last row. *(Ch 4d, p, 4d, j in next smp of same ch) 3 times, 4d, p, 4d, j in first free smp of next ch. Rep from * around. Cut and tie. FW. PW.

Grandmother's Lace

Advanced

Materials: DMC size 80 thread.

Row 1: SR 5d, p, 5d, cl. *SR 5d, p, 5d, cl. RW. Ch 7d, p, 8d, smp, 4d. RW. R 6d, j to p on last SR made, 4d, smp, 2d, cl. **¹⁄₃₂″ sp. R 2d, j to corr smp on last ring, 4d, p, 4d, smp, 2d, cl. Rep from ** 3 times. ¹⁄₃₂″ sp. R2d, j to corr p on last ring, 4d, p, 6d, cl. Total of 6 rings. RW. Ch 4d, j to corr smp on prev ch, 8d, p, 7d. RW. SR 5d, j to first p of last ring made, 5d, cl. Rep from * to desired length, SR 5d, p, 5d. Cut and tie. FW. PW.

To join ends of lace, omit last 2 SR's; join last ch bet first 2 SR.

Row 2: J thread bet first 2 SR. Ch 4, p, ch 4, *j to free p on next ring, 3d, 4 p sep by 3d, 3d.** Rep from * to ** 2 times, j to free p of next ring, 2d, p, 2d, smp, j bet next 2 SR, 2d, j to smp on prev ch, 2d, p, 2d. Rep from * across, ending with ch 4, p, ch 4, j bet last 2 SR. Cut and tie. FW. PW.

If working continuous lace, begin with ch 2, smp, ch 2, p, ch 4, work row as above; joining last ch as follows: ch 4d, p, 2d, j to first smp made, 2d, j to beginning.

Materials: DMC Cordonnet Spécial, size 30.

Row 1 (2 shuttles): *3-Ring Cluster— Sh 1:* R 8d, p, 4d, smp, 4d, cl. R 4d, j to smp of last ring, 12d, smp, 4d, cl. R 4d, j to smp of last ring, 4d, p, 8d, cl. RW. Ch 4d, smp, 8d. RW. *R 8d, j to free p on 3rd ring of last cluster, 8d, cl. RW. *Sh 2:* R

Edging #1

Intermediate

8d, p, 8d, cl. *Sh 1:* Ch 8d, smp, 4d. RW. *3-Ring Cluster—*R 8d, j to 2nd p on 3rd ring of last cluster made (same p as last joining), 4d, smp, 4d, cl. R 4d, j to smp of last ring, 12d, smp, 4d, cl. R 4d, j to smp of last ring, 4d, p, 8d, cl.† RW. Ch 4d, j to smp p of last ch, 8d. RW. Rep from * for desired length, ending last rep at †. Cut and tie. FW. PW.

Edging #2
Intermediate

Materials: DMC Cordonnet Spécial, size 30.

Row 1: *LR 6d, 5 p sep by 2d, 6d, cl. RW. Ch 8d, p, 2d, 3 p sep by 3d, 2d, p, 5d. RW. R 5d, p, 5d, cl. RW. Ch 5d, p, 2d, 3 p sep by 3d, 2d, p, 8d. RW. Rep from * to desired length. If working in a circle, j last ch to base of first ring made. For straight lace, end with LR. Cut and tie. FW. PW.

Row 2: R 3d, j to last p made on last LR, 3d, cl. RW. (Ch 2d, 3 p sep by 1d, 2d. RW. R 3d, j to next free p, 3d, cl. RW.) 4 times. *Ch 3d. RW. R 5d, j to free p on next ring, 5d, cl. RW. Ch 9d. RW. R 5d, j to same p as last ring, 5d, cl. RW. Ch 3d. † RW. R 3d, j to first free p of next ring, 3d, cl. RW. (Ch 2, 3 p sep by 1d, 2d. RW. R 3d, j to next free p, 3d, cl. RW.) 4 times. Rep from * around. If working in a circle, end at † and j last ch to base of first ring made. Cut and tie. FW. PW.

Edging #3
Beginner

Materials: DMC Cordonnet Spécial, size 30.
Be careful not to let go of the rolled sts before the ring is closed.

Row 1: *3-Ring Cluster*—R 5d, p, 1d, RSt 14, 1d, p, 5d, cl. R 5d, j to corr p on last ring, 1d, RSt 20, 1d, p, 5d, cl. R 5d, j to corr p on last ring, 1d, RSt 14, 1d, p, 5d, cl. RW. Ch 4d, p, 3d, 6 p sep by 1d, 3d. RW. *(R 5d, j to corr p on last ring, 2d, 5 p sep by 1d, 2d, p, 5d, cl. RW. Ch 3d, 6 p sep by 1d, 3d. RW.) 8 times, omitting last ch. Ch 3d, 6 p sep by 1d, 3d, p, 4d. RW. † *3-Ring Cluster*—R5d, j to corr p on last ring, 1d, RSt 14, 1d, p, 5d, cl. R 5d, j to corr p on last ring, 1d, RSt 20, 1d, p, 5d, cl. R 5d, j to corr p on last ring, RSt 14, 1d, p, 5d, cl. RW. Ch 4d, j to corr p of last ch, 3d, 6 p sep by 1d, 3d. RW. Rep from * 7 times, ending last rep at † and joining last p of last ch to first p of first ch. J last ch to base of first cluster. Cut and tie. FW. PW. Tack to front of pillow.

15

Edging #4
Intermediate

Materials: DMC Cordonnet Spécial, size 30.

Row 1: R 18d, smp, 3d, smp, 9d, cl. Ch 3d, p, 14d, p, 3d, j shuttle thread to first free smp on ring. RW. J both threads to 2nd free smp on ring. R 18d, smp, 3d, smp, 9d, cl. Ch 3d, p, 14d, p, 3d, j shuttle thread to first smp on ring. RW. J both threads to 2nd free smp on ring. *R 18d, smp, 3d, smp, 9d, cl. Ch 3d, j ch thread to corr p on corr ch, 14d, p, 3d, j shuttle thread to first smp on ring. RW. J both threads to 2nd smp on ring. Rep from * for desired length. Cut and tie. FW. PW.

Edging #5
Intermediate

Materials: DMC Cordonnet Spécial, size 30.

Row 1 (2 Shuttles): *Sh 1:* *R 8d, smp, 8d, cl. RW. Ch 12d. RW. R 8d, smp, 8d, cl. RW. Ch 5d. *Sh 2:* R 6d, 3 lp sep by 1d, 3d, smp, 3d, cl. (*Sh 1:* Ch 4d. *Sh 2:* R 3d, j to smp of prev Sh-2 ring, 3d, 3 lp sep by 1d, 3d, smp, 3d, cl.) twice *Sh 1:* Ch 4 d. *Sh 2:* R 5d, j to smp of prev Sh-2 ring, 3d, 3 lp sep by 1d, 6d, cl. *Sh 1:* Ch 5d. RW. Rep from * for desired length. R 8d, p, 8d, cl. (Directions from † to †† make a finished edge, if desired; otherwise, cut and tie.) †RW. Ch 10d. *Sh 2:* R 6d, 3 lp sep by 1d, 3d, smp, 3d, cl. (*Sh 1:* Ch 4d. *Sh 2:* R 3d, j to smp of prev Sh-2 ring, 3d, 3 lp sep by 1d, 3d, smp, 3d, cl.) twice. *Sh 1:* Ch 4d. *Sh 2:* R 3d, j to smp of prev Sh-2 ring, 3d, 3 lp sep by 1d, 6d, cl. *Sh 1:* Ch 10d. RW. †† R 8d, j to corr p on last Sh-1 ring made. Work opp side following pattern and joining Sh-1 rings to Sh-1 rings of opp side. Work from † to †† to finish edge. J last ch to base of first ring. Cut and tie. FW. PW.

Edging #6—
Hand in Hand
Intermediate

Materials: DMC Cordonnet Spécial, size 30. (Use of size 70 or 80 thread will give a more delicate edging.)

Row 1: R 5d, lp, 2d, 9 p sep by 2d, 2d, lp, 5d, cl. RW. *Ch JkS 25. RW. R 5d, j to corr lp on last ring, 2d, 9 p sep by 2d, 2d, lp, 5d, cl. RW. Rep from * for desired length. *Do not cut thread.* RW. Ch 5d, 7 p sep by 2d, 5d, **j to bottom of next ring, 5d, j to last p on prev ch, 2d, 6 p sep by 2d, 5d. Rep from ** around. J last ch to base of first ring made. Cut and tie. FW. PW.

Edging #7
Intermediate

Materials: DMC Cordonnet Spécial, size 30.

Row 1: LR 5d, 5 p sep by 3d, 5d, cl. RW. *Ch 5d, smp, 5d. RW. SR 5d, j to corr p of last ring, 6d, p, 5d, cl. RW. Ch 5d, smp, 5d. RW. LR 5d, j to corr p, 3d, 4 p sep by 3d, 5d, cl. RW. Rep from * for desired length. Cut and tie. FW. PW.
Row 2: Starting with SR, rep Row 1, join all ch's to ch's of prev row. Cut and tie. FW. PW.

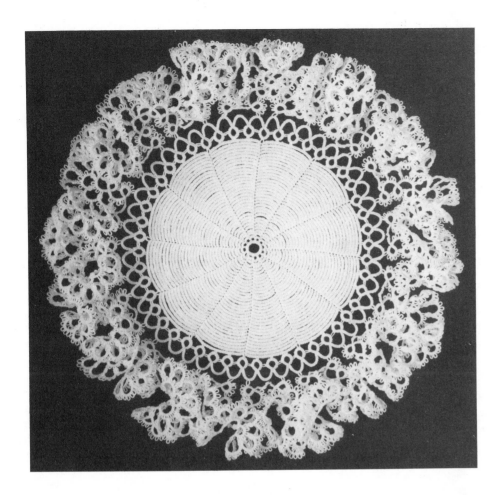

Elizabeth

Advanced
Completed size: 8 ½" diameter

Materials: DMC Cordonnet Spécial, size 30—one ball white.

Center Ring (shuttle and ball): R 2d, 12 smp sep by 3d, 1d, cl. RW. J to first p. *Do not cut thread until directed.*

Row 1: *Ch smp, 3d, j to next smp. Rep from * 11 times.
Row 2: *Ch smp, 4d, j to next smp. Rep from * 11 times.
Row 3: *Ch smp, 4d, j to next smp. Rep from * 11 times.
Row 4: *Ch smp, 5d, j to next smp. Rep from * 11 times.
Row 5: Repeat Row 4.
Rows 6–31: Work as for prev rows, increasing the number of double stitches between joins by 1 on each row. You will have 31 double stitches between joins on Row 31.
Row 32: Ch smp, *7d, smp, 8d, smp, 8d, smp, 7d, j to next smp. Rep from * 10 times. Ch smp, 7d, smp, 8d, smp, 8d, smp, 6d, smp, 1d, j to first smp of row. Cut and tie. FW. PW.
Row 33: R 4d, p, 5d, j to any smp on last row, 5d, p, 4d, cl. RW. *Ch 7d, p, 7d. RW. R 4d, j to corr p on last ring, 5d, j to next smp on last row, 5d, p, 4d, cl. RW. Ch 7d, p, 7d. RW. R 4d, j to corr p, 5d, j to next smp, 5d, p, 4d, cl. RW. Ch 14d. RW. R 4d, j to corr p, 5d, j to next smp, 5d, p, 4d, cl. RW. Rep from * around, making last ring as follows: R 4d, j to corr p, 5d, j to corr p on last row, 5d, j to first p on first ring made, 4d, cl. Last ch: 14d, j to base of first ring made. Cut and tie. FW. PW.
Row 34: R 5d, j to p on first ch made on last row, 2d, 5 p sep by 2d, 5d, cl. RW. *(Ch 3d, 5 p sep by 2d, 3d. RW. R 5d, j to last p on last ring, 2d, 5 p sep by 2d, 5d, cl. RW.) 4

times. Make ch once more. RW. R 5d, j to corr p on last ring, 2d, 4 p sep by 2d, 2d, j to corr p on next ch of last row, 5d, cl—one bridge made. RW. Ch JkS 23.† R 5d, j to next free p on last row, 2d, 5 p sep by 2d, 5d, cl. RW. Rep from * 15 times, ending last rep at †. Join in base of first ring—16 bridges made. Cut and tie. FW. PW.
Row 35: R 2d, j to 3rd p on last ch of any bridge, 2d, j to 3rd p on first ch of next bridge, 2d, cl. RW. **Ch 2d, 5 p sep by 2d, 2d. RW. *R 3d, j to first p on next ch, 3d, cl. RW. Ch 3d, 5 p sep by 2d, 3d. RW. R 3d, j to 3rd p on same ch, 3d, cl. RW. Ch 3d, 5 p sep by 2d, 3d. RW. R 3d, j to 5th p on same ch, 3d, cl. RW. Ch 3d, 5 p sep by 2d, 3d. RW. Rep from * 2 times, omitting last ch. Ch 2d, 5 p sep by 2d, 2d.† R 2d, j to 3rd p on next ch, 2d, j to 3rd p on first ch of next bridge, 2d, cl. Rep from ** 15 times, ending last rep at †. J last ch to base of first ring made. Cut and tie. FW. PW.
Row 36: Start over first ring made on last row. R 3d, j to 3rd p on last ch made on last row, 3d, cl. R 3d, j to 3rd p on next ch, 3d, cl. **Ch 3d, 5 p sep by 2d, 3d. RW. *(R 3, j to first p on next ch, 3d, cl. RW. Ch 3d, 5 p sep by 2d, 3d. RW. R 3d, j to 3rd p on same ch, 3d, cl. RW. Ch 3d, 5 p sep by 2d, 3d. RW. R 3d, j to 5th p on same ch, 3d, cl. RW. Ch 3d, 5 p sep by 2d, 3d, cl. RW.) 3 times.† R 3d, j to 2nd p on next ch, 3d, cl. RW. Ch 3d, 5 p sep by 2d, 3d. RW. R 3d, j to 4th p on same ch, 3d, cl. RW. Ch 3d, 5 p sep by 2d, 3d. RW. Rep from * twice, end last rep at †. R 3d, j to 3rd p on next ch, 3d, cl. R 3d, j to 3rd p on next ch, 3d, cl. RW. Rep from ** 15 times, ending last rep by joining last ch to first two joined rings made. Cut and tie. FW. PW.

Starburst

Intermediate
Completed size: 13½″ diameter.

Materials: DMC Cordonnet Spécial, size 30—one ball.
Use one shuttle only unless otherwise directed.

To tie rings: Insert crochet hook through left side of rings;
going under rings, hook thread from shuttle and bring it back
under, drawing up a loop. Insert shuttle through loop, pull up
tight.

Row 1: R 3d, smp, 3d, lp, 3d, smp, 3d, cl. *R 3d, j to last smp,
3d, lp, 3d, smp, 3d, cl. Rep from * 6 times, joining last p to
first p on first ring made. Cut and tie. FW. PW.

Row 2 (shuttle and ball): R 8d, j to any lp, 8d, cl. RW. *Ch
5d, 5 p sep by 2d, 5d. RW. R 8d, j to next lp, 8d, cl. Rep from
* 6 times. Ch 5d, 5 p sep by 2d, 5d, j to base of first ring
made. Cut and tie. FW. PW.

Row 3: R 3d, j to first p of any ch, 3d, cl. RW. ¼″ sp. R 6d, 3 p
sep by 6d, 6d, cl. RW. ¼″ sp. *R 3d, j to 3rd p of same ch, 3d,
cl. RW. ¼″ sp. R 6d, j to 3rd p of adj ring, 6d, p, 6d, p, 6d, cl.
RW. ¼″ sp. R 3d, j to 5th p of same ch, 3d, cl. RW. ¼″ sp. R
6d, j to 3rd p of adj ring, 6d, p, 6d, p, 6d, cl. ¼″ sp. † R
3d, j to first p of next ch, 3d, cl. RW. ¼″ sp. R 6d, j to 3rd p of
adj ring, 6d, p, 6d, p, 6d, cl. ¼″ sp. Rep from * 7 times,
ending last rep at † and joining last large ring to first large
ring. Cut and tie. FW. PW.

Row 4: *3 Ring Cluster*—R 8d, p, 8d, p, 4d, cl. R 4d, j to last
p, 9d, j to p directly over ring of 2nd row, 9d, p, 4d, cl. R 4d, j
to last p, 8d, p, 8d, cl. ¼″ sp. R 8d, j to free p of last ring, 8d,

p, 8d, cl. RW. R 10d, p, 10d, cl. Tie. ¼″ sp. RW. *R 7d, j to p
of adj ring, 3d, p, 10d, cl. RW. R 12d, p, 8d, cl. Tie. ¼″ sp.
3-Ring Cluster—R 8d, j to free p of adj ring, 8d, p, 4d, cl. R
4d, j to last p, 9d, p, 9d, p, 4d, cl. R 4d, j to last p, 8d, p, 8d, cl.
¼″ sp. R 8d, j to last p, 12d, cl. RW. R 10d, j to corr p before
cluster (see photograph), 3d, p, 7d, cl. Tie. ¼″ sp.** R 8d, j to
last p, 4d, p, 8d, cl. RW. R 10d, p, 10d, cl. RW. ¼″ sp.
3-Ring Cluster–R 8d, j to p of adj ring, 8d, p, 4d, cl. R 4d, j to
last p, 9d, skip 1 ring on Row 3, j to next ring, 9d, p, 4d, cl. R
4d, j to last p, 8d, p, 8d, cl. RW. ¼″ sp. R 10d, j to corr p before
cluster, 10d, cl. RW. R 8d, j to adj p, 4d, p, 8d, cl. Tie. ¼″ sp.
Rep from * 10 times. Rep from * to ** once. R 8d, j to last p,
4d, j to corr p on first ring made, 8d, cl. RW. R 10d, j to corr p
at beg, 10d, cl. Tie. Leave ¼″ sp and tie to base of first ring
made. Cut. FW. PW.

Row 5: R 6d, p, 6d, j to free p of any cluster, 6d, p, 6d, cl.
RW. R 6d, 4 p sep by 4d, 6d, cl. Tie. RW. ¼″ sp. †R 6d, j to
3rd p of corr ring, 5d, p, 5d, p, 6d, cl. R 6d, j to last p of
corr ring, 4d, 3 p sep by 4d, 6d, cl. Tie. RW. ¼″ sp. Rep from
* 4 times. R 6d, j to 3rd p of adj ring, 6d, j to next cluster, 6d,
p, 6d, cl. RW. R 6d, j to last p of adj ring, 4d, 3 p sep by 4d,
6d, cl. Tie. RW. ¼″ sp. Rep from † around, joining last two
rings to first 2 rings. Cut and tie. FW. PW.

Row 6: R 2d, j to any free p of last row, 2d, cl. RW. ½″ sp. R
2d, 3 p sep by 2d, 2d, cl. RW. ½″ sp. *R 2d, j to next p of last
row, 2d, cl. RW. ½″ sp. R 2d, j to last p of adj ring, 2d, p, 2d,

p, 2d, cl. RW. ½″ sp. Rep from * around, joining last outer ring to first outer ring. Leave ½″ sp; join to base of first ring. Cut and tie. FW. PW.

Row 7: *3-Ring Cluster*—R 10d, p, 10d, p, 4d, cl. R 4d, j to last p made, 10d, j to small ring on 6th row directly over cluster of Row 4, 10d, p, 4d, cl. R 4d, j to last p made on last ring, 10d, p, 10d, cl. ⅜″ sp. R 8d, j to last p made on last ring, 4d, p, 8d, cl. RW. R 8d, p, 12d, cl. Tie. RW. *¼″ sp. R 8d, j to corr p on adj ring, 4d, p, 8d, cl. RW. R 20d, cl. Tie. RW. ¼″ sp. R 8d, j to corr p on adj ring, 4d, p, 8d, cl. RW. R 12d, p, 8d, cl. Tie. ⅜″ sp. *3-Ring Cluster*—R 10d, j to corr p, 10d, p, 4d, cl. R 4d, j to corr p, 20d, p, 4d, cl. R 4d, j to corr p, 10d, p, 10d, cl. ⅜″ sp. R 8d, j to corr p, 12d, cl. RW. R 8d, j to corr p before cluster, 4d, p, 8d, cl. Tie. ¼″ sp. R 8d, j to corr p, 4d, p, 8d, cl. RW. R 20d, cl. Tie. RW. ¼″ sp. R 8d, j to corr p, 4d, p, 8d, cl. RW. R 12d, p, 8d, cl. Tie.† RW. ⅜″ sp. *3-Ring Cluster*—R 10d, j to corr p, 10d, p, 4d, cl. R 4d, j to corr p, 10d, skip 7 p's on Row 6, j to 8th p, 10d, p, 4d, cl. R 4d, j to corr p, 10d, p, 10d, cl. ⅜″ sp. R 8d, j to corr p, 4d, p, 8d, cl. RW. R 8d, j to corr p before cluster, 12d, cl. Tie. RW. Rep from * around, ending last rep at † and joining last 2 rings to corr rings at beg of row. Leave ⅜″ sp and join to base of first cluster. Cut and tie. FW. PW.

Materials: DMC Cordonnet Spécial, size 30—one ball.

Row 1 (one shuttle): R 3d, smp, 3d, ¼″ p (leave ½″ sp), 3d, smp, 3d, cl. *¹⁄₁₆″ sp. R 3d, j to corr smp, 3d, ¼″ p, 3d, smp, 3d, cl. Rep from * 5 times. ¹⁄₁₆″ sp. R 3d, j to corr p, 3d, ¼″ p, 3d, j to first smp on first ring made, 3d, cl. Leave ¹⁄₁₆″ sp, j to base of first ring made. Cut and tie. FW.

Row 2: R 5d, j to any ¼″ p on Row 1, 5d, cl. RW. Ch 3d, 5 p sep by 2 d, 3d. RW. *R 5d, j to next ¼″ p, 5d, cl. RW. Ch 3d, 5 p sep by 2d, 3d, cl. RW. Rep from * 6 times—8 rings total. J last ch to base of first ring made. Cut and tie. FW. PW.

Row 3 (one shuttle): R 3d, j to first p of any Row 2 ch, 3d, cl. RW. ⅜″ sp. R 5d, lp, 2d, 3 p sep by 2d, 2d, lp, 5d, cl—Outer Ring. RW. *⅜″ sp. R 3d, j to 3rd p on same ch, 3d, cl. RW. ⅜″ sp. R 5d, j to corr lp on last Outer Ring made, 2d, 3 p sep by 2d, 2d, lp, 5d, cl. RW. ⅜″ sp. R 3d, j to 5th p on same ch, 3d, cl. RW. ⅜″ sp. † R 5d, j to corr lp on last Outer Ring made, 2d, 3 p sep by 2d, 2d, lp, 5d, cl. RW. ⅜″ sp. R 3d, j to first p on next ch, 3d, cl. RW. ⅜″ sp. R 5d, j to corr lp on last Outer Ring made, 2d, 3 p sep by 2d, 2d, lp, 5d, cl. RW. Rep from * 6 times, then rep from * to † once more. R 5d, j to corr lp on last Outer Ring made, 2d, 3 p sep by 2d, 2d, j to corr lp on first Outer Ring made, 5d, cl. RW. Leave ⅜″† sp, j to base of first small ring made. Cut and tie. FW. PW.

Row 4: R 3d, j to first free p on any ring on last row, 3d, cl. *RW. Ch 1d, 5 p sep by 2d, 1d. RW. R 3d, j to 3rd p on same ring, 3d, cl. RW. Ch 1d, 5 p sep by 2d, 1d.† RW. R 3d, j to first p on next ring, 3d, cl. Rep from * around, ending last rep at †. J last ch to base of first ring made. Cut and tie. FW. PW.

Row 5: R 3d, j to 2nd p on any ch on last row, 3d, cl. *RW. Ch 2d, 6 p sep by 1d, 2d. RW. R 3d, j to 4th p on same ch, 3d, cl. RW. Ch 2d, 6 p sep by 1d, 2d.† RW. R 3d, j to 2nd p on next ch, 3d, cl. Rep from * around, ending last rep at †. J last ch to base of first ring made. Cut and tie. FW. PW.

Miniature Ruffles

Beginner
Completed size: 5" diameter

ELLIPSE

FREE WHEELING
INSTRUCTIONS ON PAGE 23.

Ellipse

Intermediate
Completed size: 17″ by 13″

Materials: DMC Cordonnet Spécial, size 30—one ball.

Row 1 (one shuttle): *3-Ring Cluster*—R 7d, smp, 3d, 3 p sep by 2d, 5d, smp, 5d, cl. R 5d, j to smp, 5d, 5 p sep by 2d, 5d, smp, 5d, cl. R 5d, j to smp, 5d, 3 p sep by 2d, 3d, smp, 7d, cl. Cut and tie. *R 7d, j to smp of corr ring, 3d, 3 p sep by 2d, 3d, smp, 7d, cl. RW. R 7d, smp, 3d, 3 p sep by 2d, 3d, j to corr p of adj ring (j as if joining the end of a motif to the beg), 7d, cl. Cut and tie. Rep from * 7 times. Rep 3-Ring Cluster for opposite end, joining all appropriate p's. Cut and tie. FW. PW.

Row 2 (one shuttle): Start with either end. **R 4d, p, 4d, j to first free p on first ring of cluster, 4d, p, 4d, cl. RW. ½″ sp. R 4d, p, 4d, 3 p sep by 1d, 4d, p, 4d. RW. ½″ sp. R 4d, j to 3rd p of first ring, 4d, j to 3rd p of same ring of cluster, 4d, p, 4d. RW. ½″ sp. R 4d, p, 4d, 3 p sep by 1d, 4d, p, 4d, cl. RW. ½″ sp. R 4d, p, 4d, j to first p of 2nd ring of cluster, 4d, p, 4d, cl. RW. ½″ sp. R 4d, p, 4d, 3 p sep by 1d, 4d, p, 4d, cl. RW. ½″ sp. R 4d, j to 3rd p of corr ring, 4d, j to 3rd p of same ring of cluster, 4d, p, 4d, cl. RW. ½″ sp. R 4d, p, 4d, 3 p sep by 1d, 4d, p, 4d, cl. RW. ½″ sp. R 4d, j to 3rd p of corr ring, 4d, j to 5th p of same ring of cluster, 4d, p, 4d, cl. RW. ½″ sp. R 4d, p, 4d, 3 p sep by 1d, 4d, p, 4d, cl. RW. ½″ sp. R 4d, p, 4d, j to first p of 3rd ring of cluster, 4d, p, 4d, cl. RW. ½″ sp. R 4d, p, 4d, 3 p sep by 1d, 4d, cl. RW. ½″ sp. R 4d, j to 3rd p of corr ring, 4d, j to 3rd p of same ring of cluster, 4d, p, 4d, cl. *RW. ½″ sp. R 4d, p, 4d, 3 p sep by 1d, 4d, p, 4d, cl. RW. ½″ sp. R 4d, j to 3rd p of corr ring, 4d, j to ctr p of next ring on last row, 4d, p, 4d, cl. Rep from * 7 times. RW. ½″ sp. R 4d, p, 4d, 3 p sep by 1d, 4d, p, 4d, cl. RW. ½″ sp.† Rep from ** to * for end. Rep from * to † across second side, joining last inner ring to first inner ring. Cut and tie. FW. PW.

Row 3 (2 shuttles): Start at end—R 4d, p, 4d, p, 1d, j to ctr p of outer ring directly above first and 3rd p of ctr ring of 3-Ring Cluster, 1d, p, 4d, p, 4d, cl. RW. *Sh 1: Ch 15d. 3-Ring Cluster—Sh 2: R 14d, smp, 4d, cl. R 4d, j to smp, 5d, 3 p sep by 2d, 5d, smp, 4d, cl. R 4d, j to smp, 14d, cl. Sh 1: Ch 15d. RW. (R 4d, p, 4d, p, 1d, j to ctr p of next ring of Row 2, 1d, p, 4d, p, 4d, cl. RW. Ch 6d, 5 p sep by 2d, 6d. RW.) 14 times.† R 4d, p, 4d, p, 1d, j to ctr p of next Row 2 ring, 1d, p, 4d, p, 4d, cl. Rep from * to †. Ch 15d. J to base of first ring. Cut and tie. FW. PW.

Row 4: R 4d, p, 4d, 3 p sep by 1d, 4d, p, 4d, cl. RW. Ch 6d, p, 2d, p, 2d, j to 3rd p on ch to left of 3-Ring Cluster of last row, 2d, p, 2d, p, 6d. RW. R 4d, p, 4d, 3 p sep by 1d, 4d, p, 4d, cl. RW. *Ch 16d, j to first p on ctr ring of cluster, 13d. RW. 3-Ring Cluster—R 8d, 4 p sep by 2d, 4d, smp, 4d, cl. R 4d, j to smp, 5d, 3 p sep by 2d, 5d, smp, 4d, cl. R 4d, j to smp, 4d, 4 p sep by 2d, 8d, cl. RW. Ch 13d, j to 3rd p on ctr ring of cluster, 16d. RW. **R 4d, p, 4d, 3 p sep by 1d, 4d, p, 4d, cl. RW. Ch 6d, p, 2d, p, 2d, j to 3rd p of next ch, 2d, p, 2d, p, 6d. RW.† Rep from ** 14 times omitting the last ch. Rep from * to ** once, then from ** to † 13 times. J to base of first ch. Cut and tie. FW. PW.

Row 5: Start at either end. *R 7d, j to 4th p on first ring of cluster, 7d, cl. RW. Ch 9d, 5 p sep by 2d, 9d. RW. R 7d, j to ctr p of next ring of cluster, 7d, cl. RW. Ch 9d, 5 p sep by 2d, 9d. RW. R 7d, j to first free p of next ring of cluster, 7d, cl. RW. **Ch 9d, 5 p sep by 2d, 9d. RW. R 7d, j to last p of next ring, 7d, cl. R 7d, j to first p of next ring, 7d, cl. RW. Rep from ** 2 times, then rep ch once. RW. ***R 4d, j to last p of same ring as last j, 4d, 3 p sep by 1d, 4d, j to first p of next ring, 4d, cl. RW. Ch 9d, 7 p sep by 2d, 9d. RW. Rep from *** 7 times, omitting last ch. Rep from ** to *** . RW. Rep from * to *** around the other side. J to base of first ch. Cut and tie. FW. PW.

Row 6 (one shuttle): Start at left of either end. IR 9d, p, 3d, p, 2d, j to 3rd p of ch on prev row, 2d, p, 3d, p, 9d, cl. RW. OR 9d, p, 3d, 3 p sep by 2d, 3d, p, 9d, cl. Tie as follows: insert crochet hook from left under rings and draw up thread; insert shuttle through loop and pull up snugly, knotting the thread. ¼″ sp. *R 9d, j to last p on last outer ring made, 3d, 3 p sep by 2d, 3d, p, 9d, cl. ½″ sp. 3-Ring Cluster—R 8d, p, 2d, j to last p of last ring, 2d, p, 4d, smp, 4d, cl. R 4d, j to smp, 5d, 3 p sep by 2d, 5d, smp, 4d, cl. R 4d, j to smp, 4d, 3 p sep by 2d, 8d, cl. ½″ sp. OR 9d, j to ctr p of last ring, 3d, 3 p sep by 2d, 3d, p, 9d, cl. RW. ¼″ sp. **IR 9d, p, 3d, p, 2d, j to ctr p of next ch on last row, 2d, p, 3d, p, 9d, cl. RW. OR 9d, j to corr p on last outer ring, 3d, 3 p sep by 2d, 3d, p, 9d, cl. Tie knot as before—one set made. RW. ¼″ sp. (IR 9d, j to corr p on last inner ring, 3d, 3 p sep by 2d, 3d, p, 9d, cl. RW. OR 9d, j to corr p on last outer ring, 3d, 3 p sep by 2d, 3d, p, 9d, cl. Tie as before.) twice. J inner ring of next set to ctr p of next ch. Rep from ** twice. Continue to work sets of rings as follows: Do not j next set. J next set to next ch. Do not j next set. (J next set to 3rd p of next ch; j next set to 5th p of next ch) 7 times. (Do not j next set; j next set to ctr p of next ch) twice. (Do not j next 2 sets; j next set to ctr p of next ch) 3 times. Rep from * to ** for end. Work opposite side to correspond, joining last 2 rings to first 2 rings. ¼″ sp. Cut and tie. FW. PW.

Row 7: *JK 10, j to ctr p of first single OR ring just before cluster, JK 10, cl. RW. Ch 14d, 5 p sep by 2d, 14d. RW. JK 10, j to ctr p of 2nd ring of cluster, JK 10, cl. RW. Ch 14d, 5 p sep by 2d, 14d. RW. JK 10, j to ctr p of next single OR ring, JK 10, cl. RW. Ch 14d, 5 p sep by 2d, 14d. RW. (R 8d, j to ctr p of next ring, 8d, cl. R 8d, j to ctr p of next ring, 8d, cl. RW. Ch 14d, 5 p sep by 2d, 14d. RW.) 20 times. Rep from * around. J to base of first ring. Cut and tie. FW. PW.

Row 8: Starting at end, *R 4d, p, 4d, 3 p sep by 2d, 4d, p, 4d, cl. RW. Ch 10d, p, 2d, p, 2d, j to ctr p on ch bet 3rd JK and double rings, 2d, p, 2d, p, 10d. RW. **R 4d, p, 4d, 3 p sep by 2d, 4d, p, 4d, cl. RW. Ch 10d, p, 2d, p, 2d, j to ctr p on next ch, 2d, p, 2d, p, 10d. RW. Rep from * 19 times.** Rep ring once. Ch 20d, j to ctr p of next ch, 18d. RW. 3-Ring Cluster—R 14d, p, 4d, cl. R 4d, j to p, 6d, 3 p sep by 2d, 6d, p, 4d, cl. R 4d, j to p, 14d, cl. RW. Ch 18d, j to ctr p of next ch, 20d. RW. Rep from * to ** around other side. J to base of first ring. Cut and tie. FW. PW.

Row 9: *3-Ring Cluster—R 14d, smp, 4d, cl. R 4d, j to smp, 8d, j in joining of first and 2nd rings of cluster of last row, 8d, smp, 4d, cl. R 4d, j to smp, 14d, cl. RW. Ch 15d, 5 p sep by 2d, 10d. RW. JK 8, j to ctr p of 2nd ring of cluster, JK 8, cl. RW. Ch 10d, 5 p sep by 2d, 15d. RW. Rep cluster once, joining bet 2nd and 3rd rings of Row 8 cluster. RW. Ch 20d, 5 p sep by 2d, 20d. RW. R 8d, j to 5th p of next ring, 8d, cl. R 8d, j to first p of next ring, 8d, cl. RW. Ch 15d, 5 p sep by 2d, 15d. RW. **R 8d, j to 4th p of same ring, 8d, cl. R 8d, j to first p of next ring, 8d, cl. RW. Ch 15d, 5 p sep by 2d, 15d. RW. Rep from ** 19 times, omitting last ch. Ch 20d, 5 p sep by 2d, 20d. RW. Rep from * around other side. J to base of first ring. Cut and tie. FW. PW.

Mystique

Advanced
Completed size: 6 ½" by 6 ½"

Materials: DMC Cordonnet Spécial, size 30—one ball.

Row 1: *3-Ring Cluster*—R 15d, smp, 15d, cl. R 12d, smp, 6d, smp, 12d, cl. R 15d, smp, 15d, cl. RW. Ch 2d, smp, 12d, p, 12d, smp, 2d. RW. *3-Ring Cluster*—R 15d, j to smp of prev ring, 15d, cl. R 12d, smp, 6d, smp, 12d, cl. R 15d, smp, 15d, cl. RW. Ch 2d, j to last smp of prev ch, 12d, j to center p of first ch, 12d, smp, 2d. RW. Rep from * 2 more times, joining last ring and ch to corr p's of first ring and ch. Cut and tie. FW. PW.

Row 2: *3-Ring Cluster*—R 10d, smp, 20d, cl. R 12d, p, 6d, p, 12d, cl. R 20d, smp, 10d, cl. RW. Ch 2d, smp, 12d, j to 2nd smp made on any cluster on Row 1, 12d, ¼″ p (leave ½″ sp), 6d. RW. *R 20d, j to smp on 3rd ring of last cluster made, 10d, cl. JK 8. R 15d, smp, 15d, cl. RW. Ch 20d. RW. JK 8. *Large Cluster*—R 12d, j to smp of last ring, 6d, lp, 12d, cl. JK 8. Tie to base of last ring made *(see page 18)*. R 12d, lp, 8d, lp, 8d, lp, 12d, cl. JK 8. Tie to base of last ring made. R 12d, lp, 6d, smp, 12d, cl. RW. Ch 20d. RW. R 15d, j to smp of last ring, 15d, cl. JK 8.† R 10d, smp, 20d, cl. RW. Ch 6, j to adj lp, 12d, j to first smp of next cluster on Row 1, 12d, smp, 2d. RW. *3-Ring Cluster*—R 10d, j to smp of last ring made, 20d, cl. R 12d, p, 6d, p, 12d, cl. R 20d, smp, 10d, cl. RW. Ch 2d, j to smp of last ch, 12d, j to 2nd smp on same cluster of Row 1, 12d, lp, 6d. RW. Rep from * 2 times; rep from * to † once. R 10d, j to p of first ring made, 20d, cl. RW. Ch 6, j to adj p, 12d, j to first smp of next cluster on Row 1, 12d, j to first ch, 2d. J to base of first ring. Cut and tie. FW. PW.

Row 3: *3-Ring Cluster*—R 13d, p, 2d, cl. R 2d, j to corr p, 8d, p, 8d, p, 2d, cl. R 2d, j to corr p, 6d, p, 7d, cl. RW. Ch 12d. RW. *3-Ring Cluster*—R 6d, j to corr p of last ring, 9d, p, 2d, cl. R 2d, j to corr p, 8d, 3 p sep by 8d, 2d, cl. R 2d, j to corr p, 9d, p, 6d, cl. RW. Ch 12d. RW. *3-Ring Cluster*—R 7d, j to corr p of last ring, 6d, p, 2d, cl. R 2d, j to corr p, 8d, p, 8d, p, 2d, cl. R 2d, j to corr p, 13d, cl. RW.* Ch 12d, lp, 12d, j to 2nd smp on any small cluster of last row. **RW. Ch 3d, 6 p sep by 3d, j to lp of first ring of next cluster. Ch 3d, 3 p sep by 3d, 3d, j to next lp. Ch 3d, 3 p sep by 3d, 9d. R 4d, 9 p sep by 4d, 4d, cl. J to next lp. Ch 9d, 3 p sep by 3d, 3d, join to next lp. Ch 3d, 3 p sep by 3d, 3d. J to next lp. Ch 3d, 6 p sep by 3d, 3d, j to first p of next cluster.† RW. Ch 12d, lp, 12d. Rep from * to * once. Ch 12, j to lp on corr ch, 12d, j to 2nd smp of same cluster. Rep from ** around, ending last rep at †. RW. Ch 12; j to lp of first ch, 12d. J to base of first ring. Cut and tie. FW. PW.

Row 4: R 1d, p, 1d, p, 1d, j to first p on large ring of last row, 1d, p, 1d, p, 1d, cl. RW. *(Ch 1d, 4 p sep by 1d, 1d, j to next p of large ring. Ch 1d, j to corr p of last ch, 1d, 3 p sep by 1d, 1d. RW. R 1d, p, 1d, p, 1d, j to next p of large ring, 1d, p, 1d, p, 1d, cl. RW) 4 times. Ch 1d, 3 p sep by 1d, 1d, j to first p of next ch of last row, 1d, 15 p sep by 1d, 1d, j to 3rd p of same ch and first free p of next ch of last row. Ch 1d, 3 p sep by 1d, 1d, j to next p, 1d, 3 p sep by 1d, j to next 2 p's. Ch 1d, 10 p sep by 1d, 1d, j to 3rd and 4th p, 1d, 20 p sep by 1d, 1d, j to free p of first cluster, 1d, 7 p sep by 1d, 5d, j in joining bet clusters. Ch 5d, 12 p sep by 1d, 1d, j to next free p. Ch 1d, 21 p sep by 1d, graduating p's from small to large, then back to small with #11 being the largest, 1d, j to next free p. Ch 1d, 12 p sep by 1d, 1d, j bet clusters. Ch 5d, 7 p sep by 1d, 1d, j in next free p of cluster, 1d, 20 p sep by 1d, 1d, j in 3rd and 4th p of ch of last row, 1d, 10 p sep by 1d, 1d, j to last p of same ch and first p of next ch, 1d, 3p sep by 1d, 1d, j in next p, 1d, 3 p sep by 1d, j in next 2 p's, 1d, 15 p sep by 1d, 1d, j in 3rd p of same ch, 1d. RW. R 1d, p, 1d, p, 1d, j to first p of next large ring of last row. Rep from * 3 times, omitting last ring. J last ch to base of first ring. Cut and tie. FW. RW.

Free Wheeling

Intermediate
(Shown on page 20)
Completed Size: 19″

Materials: DMC Cordonnet Spécial, size 30—one ball. Use shuttle and ball unless otherwise directed.

Center Ring (one shuttle): R 1d, 12 p sep by 3d, 2d, cl. Cut and tie. FW. PW.

Row 1: R 4d, lp (all lp will be ⅜″ long—leave ¾″ sp), 4d, cl. RW. Ch 4d, j to any p on Ctr R, 4d. RW. *R 4d, lp, 4d, cl. RW. Ch 4d, j to next p on Ctr R, 4d. RW. Rep from * around, joining last ch to base of first ring made. Cut and tie. FW. PW.

Row 2: R 4d, j to any lp of last row, 4d, cl. RW. Ch 4d, 4 smp sep by 2d, 4d. RW. *R 4d, j to next lp of last row, 4d, cl. RW. Ch 4d, 4 smp sep by 2d, 4d. RW. Rep from * around, joining last ch to base of first ring made. Cut and tie. FW. PW.

Row 3: J threads to first smp made. *Ch 12 d, j to 2nd p, 7d, smp, 7d, j to 3rd smp, 12d, j to 4th smp, 6d, j to first smp on next ch. Rep from * around, joining last ch to base of first ch made. Cut and tie. FW. PW.

Row 4: *3-Ring Cluster*—R 12d, smp, 2d, cl. R 2d, j to smp, 9d, j to any free smp on last row, 9d, smp, 2d, cl. R 2d, j to smp, 12d, cl. RW. Ch 2d, smp, 10d, p, 4d, p, 3d, p, 4d, p, 10d, smp, 2d. RW. *3-Ring Cluster*—R 12d, smp, 2d, cl. R 2d, j to smp, 9d, j to next free smp on last row, 9d, smp, 2d, cl. R 2d, j to smp, 12d, cl. RW. Ch 2d, j to last smp of last ch, 10d, p, 4d, p, 3d, p, 4d, p, 10d, smp, 2d. RW. Rep from * around, joining last ch to first ch. J to base of 3-Ring Cluster. Cut and tie. FW. PW.

Row 5: J thread to first p made on any ch of last row. *Ch 12d, j to 2nd p, 8d, smp, 8d, j to 3rd p, 12d, j to 4th p, 9d, smp, 9d, j to first p on next ch. Rep from * around, joining last ch to first ch made. Cut and tie. FW. PW.

Row 6: *3-Ring Cluster*—R 12d, smp, 2d, cl. R 2d, j to smp, 9d, j to first smp made on last row (bet clusters of Row 4), 9d, smp, 2d, cl. R 2d, j to smp, 12d, cl. RW. *Ch 14d, smp, 14d, p, 4d. RW. R 12d, j to next free p of last row, 12d, cl. RW. Ch 4d, j to corr p of last ch, 14d, smp, 14d. RW. Rep cluster, joining to next p on last row. Rep from * around, omitting last cluster. J ch to base of first 3-Ring Cluster made. Cut and tie. FW. PW.

Row 7: J thread to first smp made. *Ch 6d, 4 smp sep by 6d, 6d, j to next free p. Rep from * around. J last ch to first ch made. Cut and tie. FW. PW.

Row 8: J thread to first smp made. *Ch 4d, smp, 4d, j to 2nd smp, 4d, smp, 4d, j to 3rd smp, 4d, smp, 4d, j to 4th smp, 4d, smp, 4d, j to first p on next ch. Rep from * around. J last ch to first ch made. Cut and tie. FW. PW.

Row 9: J thread to first smp made. *(Ch 5d, smp, 5d, j in next smp) twice, 6d, smp, 6d, skip next smp, j in next smp. Rep from * around. J last ch made to base of first ch made. Cut and tie. FW. PW.

Row 10: J thread to first smp made. *Ch 5d, smp, 5d, j to next smp, (12d, j to next smp, 12d, j to next smp, 10d, j to next smp) 3 times, 12d, j to next smp, 12d, j to next smp. Rep from * around. J last ch to first ch made. Cut and tie. FW. PW.

Row 11: Make 6 motifs by repeating Ctr R and Rows 1, 2 and 3. On last row, join motifs to free p's of Row 10 of doily.

Row 12: Make 6 motifs by repeating Ctr R and Rows 1 and 2, making Ctr R with 14 p's. Rep Row 3, joining 4th smp to a Row 11 motif and 13th smp to adj Row 11 motif. Counting the join to the doily as #1, you will join to the 4th and 10th p's of Row 11 motifs—*see photograph, page 20*. Cut and tie. FW. PW.

Row 13: J thread to first free smp on left-hand side of any Row 11 motif. *Ch 30d, j to next smp, 9d, 4 smp sep by 4d, 9d, j to next smp, 9d, 4 smp sep by 4d, 9d, j to next smp, 30d, j to next smp, 7d, smp, 7d, j to first free p of next motif, (12d, 4 smp sep by 4d, 12d, j to next free p) 7 times, ch 7d, smp, 7d, j to first free p on next motif. Rep from * around. J last ch to first ch made. Cut and tie. FW. PW.

Row 14: J thread to first smp made. *Ch 14d, j to 2nd smp, 9d, smp, 9d, j to 3rd smp, 14d, j to 4th smp, 9d, j bet corr ch's of last row, 9d, j to first smp of next ch, 14d, j to 2nd smp, 9d, smp, 9d, j to 3rd smp, 14d, j to 4th smp, 9d, j bet ch's of last row, ch 30d, j in next free smp, 10d, j to first free p on next ch, (14d, j to 2nd p, 9d, smp, 9d, j to 3rd smp, 14d, j to 4th smp, 12d, j to first free p on next ch) 7 times, omitting last ch, ch 10d, j to smp, 30d, skip next join on last row; j bet next 2 ch's on last row, 9d, j to first p of next ch. Rep from * around. J last ch to first ch made. Cut and tie. FW. PW.

Bridged Ruffles

Intermediate
Completed size: 7″ diameter

Materials: DMC Cordonnet Spécial, size 30— one ball.

Row 1: R 5d, 6 p sep by 2d, 5d, cl. RW. *Ch 3d, 5 p sep by 2d, 3d. RW. R 5d, j to last p of last ring, 2d, 5 p sep by 2d, 5d, cl. RW. Rep from * 26 times, joining last p of last ring to first p of first ring. RW. Make one more ch. J ch to base of first ring made. Cut and tie. FW. PW.

Row 2: R 5d, j to 3rd p on any ch, 2d, 5 p sep by 2d, 5d, cl. RW. *(Ch 3d, 5 p sep by 2d, 3d. RW. R 5d, j to corr p on last ring made, 2d, 5 p sep by 2d, 5d, cl. RW.) 5 times. Rep ch once more. RW. R 5d, j to last ring made, 2d, 4 p sep by 2d, 2d, skip 1 ch on Row 1, j to 3rd p of next ch—1 bridge made. Ch JkS 30. Sk 1 ch. R 5d, j to 3rd p of next ch, 2d, 5 p sep by 2d, 5d, cl. Rep from * around, omitting last ring. J JkS ch to base of first ring made—7 bridges. Cut and tie. FW. PW.

Row 3: Start on the left side of any bridge. *R 3d, j to 3rd p on last ch of bridge, 3d, cl. R 3d, j to 3rd p on first ch of next bridge, 3d, cl. RW. Ch 3d, 5 p sep by 2d, 3d. RW. (R 3d, j to first p on next ch, 3d, cl. RW. Rep ch. RW. R 3d, j to 3rd p on same ch, 3d, cl. RW. Rep ch. RW. R 3d, j to 5th p on same ch, 3d, cl. RW. Rep ch. RW.) 4 times. Rep from * around 7 bridges. J last ch to base of first ring made. Cut and tie. FW. PW.

Row 4: Start on the left side of any bridge. *R 3d, j to 3rd p on last ch of bridge, 3d, cl. R 3d, j to 3rd p on first ch of next bridge, 3d, cl. RW. Ch 3d, 5 p sep by 2d, 3d. RW. **R 3d, j to first p of next ch, 3d, cl. RW. Rep ch. RW. R 3d, j to 3rd p on same ch, 3d, cl. RW. Rep ch. RW. R 3d, j to 5th p on same ch, 3d, cl. RW. Rep ch. RW.** Rep from ** to ** once. ***R 3d, j to 2nd p of next ch, 3d, cl. RW. Rep ch. RW. R 3d, j to 4th p on same ch, 3d, cl. RW. Rep ch. RW.*** (Rep from ** to ** 2 times and from *** to *** once) twice. Rep from ** to ** 2 times. Rep from * over next 7 bridges. J last ch to base of first double rings made. Cut and tie. FW. PW.

Sidekick

Intermediate
Completed size: 6¼″ diameter

Materials: DMC Cordonnet Spécial, size 30—one ball.

Row 1: R 2d, 9 p sep by 3d, 1d, cl. RW. Do not cut thread until instructed.

Row 2: *Ch smp, 4d, j in next p. Rep from * around—10 chains.

Rows 3 & 4: Rep Row 2.

Row 5: *Ch smp, 5d, j to next smp. Rep from * around.

Row 6: *Ch smp, 8d, j to next smp. Rep from * around.

Row 7: *Ch smp, 10d, j to next smp. Rep from * around.

Row 8: Rep Row 7.

Row 9: Work as for Row 8, inc'g d between joins to 12.

Row 10: Inc d to 14.

Row 11: Inc d to 16.

Row 12: *Ch smp, 16d, j to next smp. Rep from * around.

Row 13: Inc d to 18.

Rows 14, 15, & 16: *Ch smp, 18d, j to next smp. Rep from * around.

Row 17: Inc d to 20.

Row 18: Inc d to 22.

Rows 19 & 20: *Ch smp, 22d, j to next smp. Rep from * around.

Row 21: Inc d to 24.

Rows 22 & 23: *Ch smp, 24d, j to next smp. Rep from * around.

Row 24: Inc d to 26.

Row 25: *Ch smp, 26d, j to next smp. Rep from * around.

Row 26: Inc d to 28.

Row 27: Inc d to 30.

Row 28: Inc d to 32.

Row 29: Inc d to 34.

Row 30: Inc d to 36.

Row 31: *Ch smp, 7d, 4 p sep by 8d, 7d, j to next smp. Rep from * 8 times. Ch p, 7d, 4 p sep by 8d, 6d, p, 1d, j to first smp. Cut and tie. FW. PW.

Row 32: R 4d, p, 4d, j to any p on last row, 4d, p, 4d, cl. RW. *Ch 6d, smp, 6d. RW. R 4d, j to 3rd p on last ring, 4d, j to next p on last row, 4d, p, 4d, cl. RW. Rep from * around, ch 6d, p, 6d. J ch to base of first ring made. Cut and tie. FW. PW.

Row 33: J thread to any smp on last row. *Ch smp, 10d, j to next free smp. Rep from * around. *Do not cut thread.*

Rows 34 & 35: *Ch smp, 10d, j to next smp on last row. Rep from * around. *Do not cut thread.*

Row 36: *Ch 10d, j to next smp on last row. Rep from * around. J last ch to base of first ch made. Cut and tie. FW. PW.

TRIANGLE RING

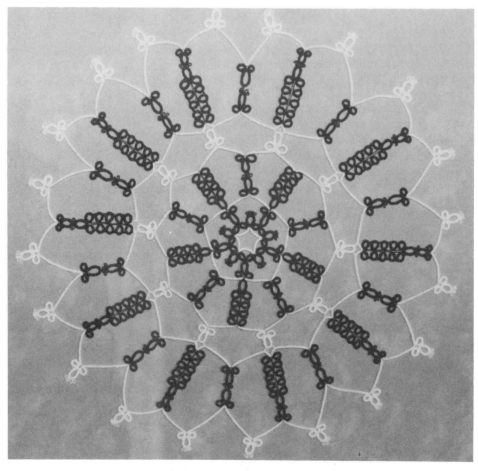

KALEIDOSCOPE

Triangle Ring

Advanced
Completed size: 12″ diameter

Materials: DMC Cordonnet Spécial, size 30—one ball; 12″ metal ring; triangular crystal with hole for hanging; transparent nylon thread; needle.

First Medallion: R 4d, 3 p sep by 4d, 4d, cl. RW. Ch 5d, 3 p sep by 4d, 5d. RW. *R 4d, j to last p on first ring made, 4d, p, 4d, p, 4d, cl. RW. Ch 4d, 3 p sep by 4d, 5d. RW. Rep from * 6 times, joining first p on last ring to corr p on first ring made. J last ch to base of first ring made. Cut and tie. FW. PW.
2nd Medallion: Work as for First Medallion, joining 2nd p on first ch to 2nd p on any ch of first medallion made.
3rd Medallion: Work as for First Medallion, joining 2nd p on first ch to 2nd p on 7th ch of 2nd medallion made, 2nd p on 2nd ch to 8th ch of 2nd medallion made and 2nd p on 3rd ch to adj ch on first medallion made. Cut and tie. FW.

Make 3 more medallions, joining them to each other and to prev medallions as in photograph. One triangle is now complete. Make two more triangles, joining as in the photograph.

Using nylon thread, sew between stitches of center ring in base of any triangle *(see photograph)*. Loop thread through hole in prism; knot thread over prism. Sew thread up other side of ring. Cut and tie.

Crochet around metal ring. Center tatted triangle in center of ring, sew to covering of ring. Cut and tie.

Kaleidoscope

Beginner
Completed size: 13″ diameter

Materials: DMC Cordonnet Spécial, size 30—one ball each two different colors. This doily is made with 2 shuttles wound with different colors of thread. In the sample shown, shuttle 1 is wound with black and shuttle 2 with white. Use white for the ball thread.

Row 1: *3-Ring Cluster*—R 9d, p, 5d, smp, 4d, cl. R 4d, j to smp of last ring, 8d, 5 p sep by 1d, 8d, smp, 4d, cl. R 4d, j to smp of last ring, 5d, p, 9d, cl. RW. Ch 15d. RW. *3-Ring Cluster*—R 9d, j to p of last ring, 5d, smp, 4d, cl. R 4d, j to smp, 8d, 5 p sep by 1d, 8d, smp, 4d, cl. R 4d, j to smp, 5d, p, 9d, cl. RW. Ch 15d. RW. Rep from * 3 times, joining last p of last ring to first p on first ring made and ch to base of first ring made. Cut and tie. FW. PW.
Row 2: *Inner Cluster*—R 14d, smp, 4d, cl. R 4d, j to smp, 12d, j to joining bet 2 adj clusters of prev row, 12d, smp, 4d, cl. R 4d, j to smp, 14d, cl. RW. Ch 25d. *Outer Cluster*—R 15d, smp, 4d, cl. R 4d, j to smp, 10d, 5 p sep by 1d, 10d, smp, 4d, cl. R 4d, j to smp, 15d, cl. Ch 25d. RW. Rep from * 4 times. J last ch to base of first ring made. Cut and tie. FW. PW.
Row 3 (2 shuttles): *Sh 1:* R 13d, p, 8d, cl. ¼″ sp. (R 8d, j to last p, 5d, p, 8d, cl. ¼″ sp.) twice. R 8d, j to last p, 11d, p, 4d, cl. R 4d, j to last p, 12d, j bet first and 3rd rings of Inner Cluster of last row, 12d, p, 4d, cl. R 4d, j to last p, 11d, p, 8d, cl. (¼″ sp. R 8d, j to last p, 5d, p, 8d, cl.) twice. ¼″ sp. Insert a crochet hook from the right side of the next ¼″ sp, draw up a loop and pass the shuttle through it, connecting the shuttle thread to the base of the first ring. R 8d, j to last p, 13d, cl. RW. Ch 25d. *Sh 2: 3-Ring Cluster*—R 15d, p, 4d, cl. R 4d, j to last p, 8d, p, 5d, p, 8d, p, 4d, cl. R 4d, j to last p, 15d, cl. *Sh 1:* Ch 25d. RW. R 15d, p, 4d, cl. R 4d, j to last p, 13d, j to 3rd p of next Outer Cluster of last row, 13d, p, 4d, cl. R 4d, j to last p, 15d, cl. RW. Ch 25d, *Sh 2: 3-Ring Cluster*—R 15d, p, 4d, cl. R 4d, j to last p, 8d, p, 5d, p, 8d, p, 4d, cl. R 4d, j to last p, 15d, cl. *Sh 1:* Ch 25d. Rep from * 4 times. Join ch to base of first rings made. Cut and tie. FW. PW.
Row 4: *R 15d, p, 8d, cl. ¼″ sp. (R 8d, j to last p, 7d, p, 8d, cl. ¼″ sp.) 3 times. R 8d, j to free p, 11d, p, 4d, cl. R 4d, j to last p, 12d, p, 12d, p, 4d, cl. R 4d, j to last p, 11d, p, 8d, cl. (¼″ sp. R 8d, j to last p, 7d, p, 8d, cl.) 3 times. ¼″ sp, j to base of first ring as in Row 3. R 8d, j to free p, 15d, cl. RW. Ch 6d, j to 2nd p of Sh-2 3-Ring Cluster on Row 3, 29d. RW. *3-Ring Cluster*—R 15d, p, 4d, cl. R 4d, j to last p, 12d, 5 p sep by 1d, 12d, p, 4d, cl. R 4d, j to last p, 15d, cl. RW. Ch 29d, j to first p of next cluster, 6d. RW. Rep from * 9 times. J ch to base of first ring. Cut and tie. FW. PW.
Row 5 (2 shuttles): *Sh 1: 3-Ring Cluster*—R 15d, p, 4d, cl. R 4d, j to last p, 16d, j to ctr p of 3-Ring Cluster on Row 4, 16d, p, 4d, cl. R 4d, j to last p, 15d, cl. RW. Ch 40d. *Sh 2: 3-Ring Cluster*—R 15d, p, 4d, cl. R 4d, j to last p, 8d, 5 p sep by 1d, 8d, p, 4d, cl. R 4d, j to last p, 15d, cl. *Sh 1:* Ch 30d. RW. *3-Ring Cluster*—R 10d, p, 4d, cl. R 4d, j to last p, 6d, p, 1d, p, 1d, j to free p on next motif of Row 4, 1d, p, 1d, p, 6d, p, 4d, cl. R 4d, j to last p, 10d, cl. RW. Ch 30d. *Sh 2: 3-Ring Cluster*—R 15d, p, 4d, cl. R 4d, j to last p, 8d, 5 p sep by 1d, 8d, p, 4d, cl. R 4d, j to last p, 15d, cl. *Sh 1:* Ch 40d. Rep from * 9 times. J ch to base of first ring. Cut and tie. FW. PW.

Variation: To make center without the chain, work Row 1 as follows:
3-Ring Cluster—R 9d, p, 5d, smp, 4d, cl. R 4d, j to smp of last ring, 8d, 5 p sep by 1d, 8d, smp, 4d, cl. R 4d, j to smp of last ring, 5d, p, 9d, cl. ½ sp. *3-Ring Cluster*—R 9d, j to p of last ring, 5d, smp, 4d, cl. R 4d, j to smp of last ring, 8d, 5 p sep by 1d, 8d, smp, 4d, cl. R 4d, j to smp of last ring, 5d, p, 9d, cl. ½ sp. RW. Rep from * 3 times, j last p to first p on first ring made and ch to base of first ring made. Cut and tie. FW. PW. Complete doily as before.

Christmas Ornaments

All bulbs use DMC Cordonnet Spécial, size 30. One ball will make several bulbs.

#1

#1

Intermediate
1⅝″-diameter clear glass Christmas bulb.

Row 1: R 4d, 3 p sep by 4d, 4d, cl. *Ch 18d. RW. *3-Ring Cluster*—R 5d, 3 p sep by 5d, 5d, cl. R5d, j corr p on last ring made, 4d, 7 p sep by 1d, 4d, p, 5d, cl. R 5d, j to corr p on last ring, 2 p sep by 5d, 5d, cl. RW. Ch 18d. RW. R 4d, j to 3rd p of adj ring, 4d, 2 p sep by 4d, 4d, cl. RW. Rep from * 6 times, omitting last ring and joining 3rd p of 7th ring to first p on first ring made. J last ch to base of first ring made. Cut and tie. FW.

Row 2: J to 4th p of ctr ring of 3-Ring Cluster. *Ch 16d, p, 16d, j to 4th p on ctr ring of next cluster. Rep from * 6 times. J to beg of first ch made. Cut and tie. FW. Place piece over bulb. Finish with weave stitch.

#2

Advanced
1⅞″-diameter clear glass Christmas bulb.

Row 1 (2 shuttles): *Sh 1:* R 3d, 7 p sep by 1d, 3d, cl. RW. *Ch 1d, 20 tp sep by 1d, 1d, twist ch 10 times. *Sh 2:* R 1d, 9 p sep by 1d, 1d, cl. *Sh 1:* Ch 1d, 20 tp sep by 1d, 1d, twist ch 10 times. RW. R 3d, j to last p of adj ring, 1d, 6 p sep by 1d, 3d, cl. RW. Rep from * 7 times, joining last ring to first ring. Ch 1d, 20 tp sep by 1d, 1d, twist ch 10 times. J ch to base of first ring made. Cut and tie. FW. Twist ch's once, making them cross over each other.

Row 2: *R 3d, 5 p sep by 1d, 3d, cl. RW. Ch 1d, 8 tp sep by 1d, 1d, twist ch 4 times, j to 5th p of any Sh-2 ring of Row 1, ch 1d, 8 tp sep by 1d, 1d, twist ch 4 times. RW. Rep from * 8 times, j ch to beg ring. Cut and tie. FW. Place piece over bulb. Finish with weave stitch.

#2

#3

#3

Intermediate
2″ diameter clear Christmas bulb.

Row 1: R 4d, 3 p sep by 4d, 4d, cl. *RW. Ch 3d, 5 p sep by 3d, 3d. *3-Ring Cluster*—R 5d, 3 p sep by 5d, 5d, cl. R 5d, j to last p of last ring, 4d, 7 p sep by 1d, 4d, p, 5d, cl. R 5d, j to corr p on last ring, 5d, 2 p sep by 5d, 5d, cl. Ch 3d, 5 p sep by 3d, 3d.† RW. R 4d, j to last p of adj ring, 4d, 2 p sep by 4d, 4d, cl. RW. Rep from * 6 times, ending last rep at † and joining last ring to first ring. J last ch to base of first ring. Cut and tie. FW.

Row 2 (2 shuttles): J to 4th p of ctr ring on cluster. **Sh 1:** Ch 3d, 5 p sep by 3d, 3d. *Sh 2:* R 4d, p, 4d, cl. *Sh 1:* Ch 3d, 5 p sep by 3d, 3d, j to 4th p of ctr ring of next cluster. Rep from * 6 times. Join to beg of first ch made. Cut and tie. FW. Place piece over bulb. Finish with weave stitch.

#4

#5

#4

Intermediate

2″ diameter clear glass Christmas bulb.

Row 1 (2 shuttles): *Sh 1:* R 5d, 3 p sep by 5d, 5d, cl. RW. Ch 8d, p, 8d. RW. *Sh 2: 3-Ring Cluster*—R 18d, smp, 2d, cl. R 2d, j to smp of last ring, 2d, 3 p sep by 1d, 2d, smp, 2d, cl. R2d, j to last p of last ring, 18d, cl. *Sh 1:* Ch 8d, p, 8d. RW. R 5d, j to last p of last Sh-1 ring, 5d, 2 p sep by 5d, 5d, cl. RW. Ch 8d, j to p of prev ch, 8d. Rep from * 6 times, joining last ring to first ring. Rep cluster. Ch 8d, j to first ch, 8d. J to base of first ring. Cut and tie. FW.

Row 2 (2 shuttles): *Sh 1:* R 18d, smp, 2d, cl. R 2d, j to smp of last ring, 2d, p, 1d, j to ctr p of ctr ring of cluster on last row, 1d, p, 2d, smp, 2d, cl. R 2d, j to corr smp of last ring, 18d, cl. RW. Ch 8d, p, 8d. *Sh 2:* R 4d, p, 4d, cl. Ch 8d, p, 8d. Rep from * around. J to base of first ring made. Cut and tie. FW. Place piece over bulb. Finish with weave stitch.

#5

Advanced

2″ diameter clear glass Christmas bulb.

Row 1 (one shuttle): R 2d, 3 p sep by 2d, 2d, cl. RW. ¼″ sp. R 4d, p, 4d, smp, 4d, p, 4d, cl. RW. *¼″ sp. R 2d, j to last p of prev ring, 2d, p, 2d, p, 2d, cl. RW. ¼″ sp. R 4d, j to last p of corr ring, 4d, smp, 4d, p, 4d, cl. Rep from * 14 times, joining last 2 rings to first 2 rings. ¼″ sp. J to base of first ring. Cut and tie. FW.

Row 2 (2 Shuttles): J thread in any joining bet large rings of prev row. *Sh 1:* Ch 3d, p, 1d, p, 1d. *Sh 2:* JK 10, cl. *Sh 1:* Ch 1d, p, 1d, p, 3d, j to next join. Rep from * 15 times. Cut and tie.

Row 3 (2 Shuttles): J thread in last p of one ch and first p of next ch. *Sh 1:* Ch 7d. *Sh 2:* R 4d, p, 4d, cl. *Sh 1:* Ch 7. J in last p of same ch and first p of next ch. Rep from * 15 times. Join last ch to beg. Cut and tie. FW.

Row 4: *R 4d, j to p of ring on last row, 4d, cl. RW. Ch 1d, 13 smp sep by 1d, 1d, twist ch 7 times. Rep from * around. Join last ch to first ring made. Cut and tie. FW.

Row 5 (2 Shuttles): J thread in ctr p of last ch made. *Sh 1:* Ch

1d, 4 smp sep by 1d, 1d, twist ch 2 times. RW. *Sh 2:* JK 8. *Sh 1:* Ch 1, 4 smp sep by 1d, 1d, twist ch 2 times. J in ctr p of next ch. Ch 1d, 9 smp sep by 1d, 1d, twist ch 3 times. *Sh 2:* R 3d, p, 3d, cl. *Sh 1:* Ch 1d, 9 smp sep by 1d, 1d, twist ch 3 times. J in ctr p of next ch. Rep from * around. J last ch to base of first ch. Cut and tie. FW. Place piece over bulb. Finish with weave stitch.

Note: JK's on 2nd row and short ch's with JK's should stick out—run your finger under them and lift.

#6

#6

Intermediate

2⅛″-diameter clear glass Christmas bulb.

R 6d, p, 3d, 4 p sep by 1d, 3d, p, 6d. JK 30. RW. Ch 18d, 3 p sep by 3d, 18d. RW. *LR 8d, 15 p sep by 1d, 8d, cl. R 5d, RSt 15, 5d, cl. RW. Ch 18d, 3 p sep by 3d, 18d. RW. R 6d, j to last p of adj ring, 3d, 4 p sep by 1d, 3d, 6d, cl. JK 30. RW. Ch 18d, p, 3d, j to corr p, 3d, p, 18d. Rep from * 5 times, joining last ring at top to first ring made. Cut and tie. FW. Place piece over bulb. Finish with weave stitch, joining thread in ctr p's of large rings. The JK's and roll stitch rings should stick out.

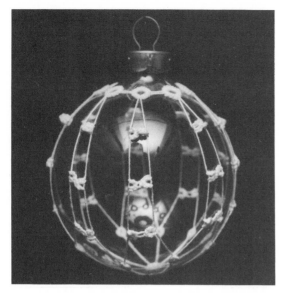

#7

#7

Intermediate
2½″-diameter glass Christmas bulb.

One shuttle: LR 3d, lp, 6d, lp, 3d, cl. RW. ½″ sp. (SR 2d, p, 2d, cl. ½″ sp.) 3 times. JK 8, p, JK 8, cl. ½″ sp. (SR 2d, p, 2d, cl. ½″ sp.) 3 times. *LR 3d, j to corr lp on adj LR, 6d, lp, 3d, cl. RW. ½″ sp. (SR 2d, j to corr p on corr SR, 2d, cl. ½″ sp.) 3 times. JK 8, p, JK 8, cl. ½″ sp. (SR 2d, p, 2d, cl. ½″ sp.) 3 times. RW. Rep from * 7 times, joining all corr p's, and joining last LR to first LR. Cut and tie. FW. Slip piece over bulb. Finish with weave stitch.

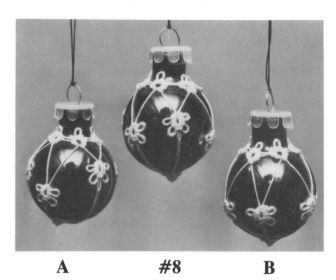

A   **#8**   **B**

#8

Beginner
1″ diameter glass Christmas bulb.

One shuttle: *R 3d, 3 p sep by 2d, 3d, cl. RW. ½″ sp. R 2d, p, 2d, 3 p sep by 1d, 2d, p, 2d, cl. RW. ½″ sp. R 3d, j to last p of corr ring, 2d, p, 2d, p, 3d, cl. RW. ¼″ sp. R 2d, p, 2d, 3 p sep by 1d, 2d, p, 2d, cl. RW. ¼″ sp. Rep from * 2 times, joining all corr p's. Cut and tie. FW. Slip piece over bulb. Finish off with weave st.

Variation A: Work rings as before, leaving ½″ sp before and after 2nd ring, ¼″ sp before and after 4th ring and ⅛″ sp before and after 6th ring. Rep from * once.
Variation B: Work as above leaving ½″ for all spaces.

#9

Intermediate
2½″-diameter clear glass Christmas bulb.

Note: All lp's are ¼″ long.
Row 1 (2 shuttles): *Sh 1:* SR 5d, lp, 3d, 3 p sep by 1d, 3d, lp, 5d, cl. RW. *Ch 1d, 30 smp sep by 1d, 1d, twist ch 8 times. *Sh 2:* LR 3d, 7 p sep by 2d, 3d, cl. LR 3d, 7 p sep by 2d, 3d, cl. *Sh 1:* Ch 1d, 30 smp sep by 1d, 1d, twist ch 8 times.† RW. LR 5d, j to corr p, 3d, 3 p sep by 1d, lp, 5d, cl. RW. Rep from * 7 times, ending last rep at † and joining last Sh-1 ring to first Sh-1 ring. J last ch to base of first ring. Cut both shuttle threads 2″ long. Tie and knot close to work. FW. Twist LR's once before joining Row 2.
Row 2 (2 shuttles): *Sh 2:* *SR 3d, 3 p sep by 2d, 2d, j to 7th p of one LR and first p on adj LR of last row, 2d, 3 p sep by 2d, 3d, cl. *Sh 1:* Ch 1d, 20 smp sep by 1d, 1d, twist ch 6 times. RW. R 2d, 5 p sep by 2d, 2d, cl. Ch 1d, 20 p sep by 1d, 1d. RW.* Rep from * to * around. Cut both shuttle threads 2″ long. Tie a knot close to work. FW. Place piece over bulb. Use weave stitch to attach at bottom of bulb, twisting lower rings once before joining.

#9

#10

Beginner

1⅝″-diameter clear glass Christmas bulb.

Row 1: R 4d, smp, 4d, p, 4d, smp, 4d, cl. RW. ¼″ sp. R 6d, p, 6d, 3p sep by 1d, 6d, p, 6d, cl. RW. *¼″sp. R 4d, j to last p of adj ring, 4d, p, 4d, p, 4d, cl. RW. ¼″ sp. R 6d, j to last p of corr ring, 6d, 3 p sep by 1d, 6d, p, 6d, cl. RW. Rep from * 9 times. ¼″ sp. J to base of first ring. Cut and tie. FW.

Row 2: R 8d, p, 8d, p, 1d, j to ctr p on last large ring of first row, 1d, p, 8d, p, 8d, cl. RW. ½″ sp. R 6d, p, 6d, 3 p sep by 1d, 6d, p, 6d, cl. RW. ½″ sp. *R 8d, j to last p of corr ring, 8d, p, 1d, j to corr p on last row, 1d, p, 8d, p, 8d, cl. RW. ½″ sp. R 6d, p, 6d, 3 p sep by 1d, 6d, p, 6d, cl. Rep from * around. ½″ sp. J to base of first ring. Cut and tie. FW. Slip piece over bulb. Join bottom with weave stitch as follows—twist lower rings 3 times. Join thread to first p of one ring and 5th p on corr ring. Once there is only single ring left, j as beginning.

#10

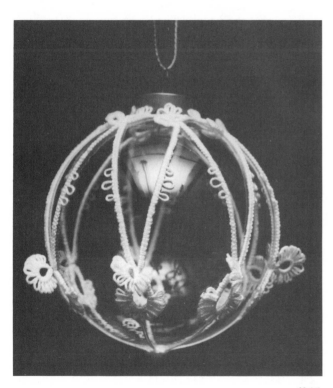

#11

#11

Intermediate

2⅝″-diameter clear glass Christmas bulb.

R 8d, p, 3d, 4 p sep by 1d, 3d, p, 8d, cl. JK 30. RW. *Ch 25d, 3 p sep by 4d, 20d. *LR 10d, 21 p sep by 1d, 10d, cl. R 3d, 17 p sep by 1d, 3d, cl. Ch 20d, 3 p sep by 4d, 25d. RW.† R 8d, j to last p of adj ring, 3d, 4 p sep by 1d, 3d, p, 8d, cl. JK 30. RW. Rep from * 6 times. Cut and tie. FW. Slip piece over bulb. Finish with weave stitch.

#12

Beginner

1″-diameter glass Christmas bulb.

One shuttle: LR 1d, smp, 2d, p, 2d, smp, 2d, p, 2d, smp, 1d, cl. RW. ½″ sp. R 4d, ¼″ lp, 4d, cl. RW. ½″ sp. *LR 1d, smp, 2d, j, 2d, smp, 2d, p, 2d, smp, 1d, cl. RW. ½″ sp. R 4d, ¼″ lp, 4d. ½″ sp. RW. Rep from * 5 times, joining last LR to first LR. Cut and tie. FW. Slip piece over bulb. Finish with weave stitch.

#13

Beginner

1″-diameter glass Christmas bulb.

Note: On all ch's, graduate the p's, increasing p's 1–6 in size, then decreasing 7–11 in size.

Row 1: R 2d, 7 p sep by 2d, 2d, cl. RW. Ch 2d, 11 graduated p sep by 1d, 2d. *RW. R 2d, p, 2d, j to corr p on last ring, 2d, 5 p sep by 2d, 3d, cl. RW. Ch 2d, 11 graduated p sep by 1d, 2d. Rep from * 6 times. J ch to base of first ring made. Cut and tie. FW.

Row 2: J to 11th p of one ch and first p of next ch. *Ch 2d, 11 graduated p's sep by 1d, 2d. J to first p of same ch and 11th p of next ch. Rep from * around. J to beg. Cut and tie. FW. Slip piece over bulb. Use weave stitch to attach at the bottom of the bulb, joining in ctr p of ch's and leaving every other ch free.

#12   **#13**

#14

#15  **#16**

#14

Intermediate
1⅞″-diameter glass Christmas bulb.

Row 1 (one shuttle): R 3d, p, 3d, ⅜″ lp, 3d, p, 3d, cl. ⅛″ sp. *R 3d, j to corr p, 3d, ⅜″ lp, 3d, p, 3d, cl. ⅛″ sp. Rep from * 6 times, joining last ring to first ring. ⅛″ sp. J to base of first ring made. Cut and tie. FW.
Row 2: *R 6d, j to lp on last row, 6d, cl. RW. Ch 5d, 5 p sep by 2d, 5d. Rep from * 7 times. J to base of first ring. Cut and tie. FW.
Row 3 (one shuttle): *R 3d, j to 2nd p on any ch of last row, 3d, cl. RW. ⁹⁄₁₆″ sp. *R 2d, 5 p sep by 1d, 2d, cl. RW. ⁹⁄₁₆″ sp. R 3d, j to 4th p on same ch, 3d, cl. ½″ sp.† R 3d, j to 2nd p on next ch, 3d cl. ⁹⁄₁₆″ sp. Rep from * 7 times, ending last rep at †. J to base of first ring. Cut and tie. FW. Place piece over bulb. Finish with weave stitch.

#15

Beginner
1″-diameter glass Christmas bulb.

R 1d, smp, 2d, p, 2d, smp, 2d, p, 2d, smp, 1d, cl. RW. ½″ sp. R 2d, p, 1d, smp, 1d, p, 1d, smp, 1d, p, 2d, cl. RW. ½″ sp. *R 1d, smp, 2d, j to corr p on adj ring, 2d, smp, 2d, p, 2d, smp, 1d, cl. RW. ½″ sp. R 2d, p, 1d, smp, 1d, p, 1d, smp, 1d, p, 2d, cl. RW. ½″ sp. Rep from * 5 times, joining last ring at top to first ring made. Cut and tie. FW. Slip piece over bulb. Finish with weave stitch.

#16

Beginner
1″-diameter glass Christmas bulb.

R 2d, 4 p sep by 2d, 2d, cl. RW. ½″ sp. R 1d, 5 p sep by 1d, 1d, cl. RW. *½″ sp. R 2d, j to corr p on adj ring, 2d, 3 p sep by 2d, 2d, cl. RW. ½″ sp. R 2d, 3 p sep by 2d, 2d, cl. RW. ½″ sp. R 2d, j to corr p, 2d, 3 p sep by 2d, 2d, cl. RW. ½″ sp. R 1d, 5 p sep by 1d, 1d, cl. RW. Rep from * once (5 total). **½″ sp. R 2d, j, 2d, p, 2d, p, 2d, j to first ring made, 2d, cl. RW. ½″ sp. R 2d, 3 p sep by 2d, 2d, cl. ½″ sp. J to base of first ring. Cut and tie. FW. Place piece over bulb. Finish with weave stitch.

PHOTOGRAPH BY KRISTINE AMUNDSON

About the Author

At the age of eight, Janet Carroll was taught to tat by her grandmother. Since then she has developed a business as a master tatter and folk artist, and has received recognition for her work from the South Dakota Arts Council and the South Dakota Cultural and Heritage Center. In addition to teaching classes for tatters at all levels of experience, she has given numerous demonstrations at museums and art centers. She is married and has two children, a girl and a boy.